CRISIS

Alan Bollard

CRISIS

ONE CENTRAL BANK GOVERNOR &
THE GLOBAL FINANCIAL COLLAPSE

ALAN BOLLARD

WITH SARAH GAITANOS

Auckland University Press

First published 2010

Auckland University Press
University of Auckland
Private Bag 92019
Auckland 1142
New Zealand
www.auckland.ac.nz/aup

ISBN 978 1 86940 469 7

National Library of New Zealand Cataloguing-in-Publication Data
Bollard, Alan.
Crisis : one Central Bank governor and the global financial
collapse / Alan Bollard with Sarah Gaitanos.
ISBN 978-1-86940-469-7
1. Global Financial Crisis, 2008-2009. 2. Finance—
Government policy—New Zealand. 3. New Zealand—
Foreign economic relations. I. Title. II. Gaitanos, Sarah.
330.90511—dc 22

Cover photograph by Ross Giblin, © *Dominion Post*
Cover design: Spencer Levine

Printed by Printlink Ltd, Wellington

CONTENTS

Sarah Gaitanos switched off the digital recorder. 'We've recorded just over twelve hours,' she said. We looked at each other across the table. 'There's a fascinating book in there.' It was September 2009. Over the past eleven months we had recorded my account of the global financial crisis of 2007 to 2009 for the Reserve Bank oral history archives.

Sarah had originally suggested the idea to Liz Castle, the Reserve Bank's Knowledge Centre manager. They saw the value of recording people's actions and responses to the crisis as it occurred, and thought that my experience as governor would be of interest. They wanted to tell not only the economic and financial story but also to show the human face of central banking. I resisted the idea at first. As the markets closed up around us, we had enough to do without worrying about a record for history. Furthermore, there were times when I did not see how this crisis could be resolved without spilling a lot of blood. In the fog of war, generals do not start writing their reminiscences. Or would these recordings be more like a captain keeping the ship's log? Or – more ominously – a black box in an aircraft to be analysed after the crash?

I was eventually persuaded, and we began. The interviews were soon capturing experiences and raw emotions: worry, angst, occasional expletives. In parts the transcripts read less like an official history and more like a teenager's diary. I sometimes found the recording sessions tense, sometimes cathartic. I felt at the time that they helped me put a narrative on the events and clarify the logic of our responses.

It was another matter when we came to write the book in the first half of 2010. The interviews certainly carried the emotions of the events as they were happening, but we discovered that they were not always reliable about cause and effect – or even sequence of events. We rewrote – adding new material, checking and restructuring – but also tried to keep a sense of real-time drama.

Keeping a record is one thing, but what is a central bank governor doing writing and publishing a book like this, while still in office, while the events are still unfolding? The answer should become apparent in the story that follows. I have had a unique vantage point from which to observe a crisis that should never have happened, to watch the desperate struggle to contain it offshore and, in some way, to assist the efforts to limit its impact on New Zealand.

Observer and participant history brings its own perils. This book does not purport to be the 'authorised version' – there are now many publications available on the crisis and this is my own story. It is not the official view of the Reserve Bank of New Zealand. However, I have had privileged access to people and information, though meetings and discussions that were carried out confidentially have remained so in these pages. Many people – ministers, senior Treasury officials and senior bankers – play crucial roles in the account that follows, and some of them will see things differently. I also had the advantage of many skilled and committed employees in the Reserve Bank of New Zealand working to alleviate the crisis. Again, some may interpret these events differently.

I have also tried to be scrupulous to ensure that I have written nothing on New Zealand that could not have been made public under the Official Information Act; indeed, much of the official policy is already in the public arena. This means that at times the book is less revealing than it might otherwise be. We hope it is no less insightful and interesting.

Crisis aims to provide an accessible account for the lay reader. To achieve this we have tried to minimise use of technical terms, economic data and references. Terminology is New Zealand usage unless otherwise specified. Those seeking clarification or more detail may wish to consult the Reserve Bank of New Zealand's website at www.rbnz.govt.nz. A list of further reading on the crisis may be found on page 194.

To paraphrase Einstein, I hope we have tried to make the story as simple as possible but no simpler.

This book was jointly written by my co-author, Sarah Gaitanos, and me. I am indebted to Sarah for her enthusiasm and skill in recording, abstracting, drafting, organising, rewriting, liaising with the publisher and indexing. She has willingly worked around my difficult timetable to help us both meet what looked like impossible deadlines.

I worked on the manuscripts mainly by hand, grabbing time when I could outside my day job. Much of the book was written in late-night or weekend sessions, at airports, on turbulent planes, in hotel rooms. This is not conducive to good handwriting. For transcribing my almost indecipherable script and organising the many drafts, I wish to thank Sandy Anderson, who worked long hours to help put the book together. Many thanks also to Alisa Maxted for typing support; Liz Castle for pushing me to do the interviews; and Elaine Little for transcribing the oral recordings. For data and interpretation I thank Rochelle Barrow, Kirdan Lees, Bevan Cook and other economics staff, as well as Victoria Zhang and David Drage. Special thanks to Grant Spencer, who gave me detailed comments, advice and explanations of what really happened; Ian Harrison for his oversight; Arthur Grimes for guidance; Don Abel for overall help in handling the book; Gary Hawke for many comments; Nick McBride for legal advice; Mike Hannah for assistance with key audiences; and John McDermott for helping me understand the big economic picture.

I wish to thank Sam Elworthy, Anna Hodge, Katrina Duncan, Vani Sripathy and Christine O'Brien of Auckland University Press for swift, supportive and skilful publishing and marketing. Thanks to Radio New Zealand's concert programmes for aural support, and Tony and Reuben's no-name coffee shop for caffeine. I thank Jenny Morel for ideas; I am also grateful to many others outside the Bank who cannot be thanked by name. Royalties from this book will be donated to charity.

In his autobiography, *The Age of Turbulence*, Alan Greenspan writes, 'There are errors in this book. I do not know where they are. If I did they would not be there. But with close to two hundred thousand words, my probabilistic mind tells me some are wrong. My apologies in advance.' The same applies to me, except that our book is shorter.

Once in a career, an event happens that tests all one's skills and all one's experience. For me, this was the event. We hope you appreciate the story.

Alan Bollard, May 2010

CHAPTER 1

The End of the Golden Weather
The Background, 1987–2007

The peaks of the Grand Tetons are sharp against the Wyoming sky. Below the mountain range, moose and elk graze the rolling grasslands and bears wander freely; in the Snake River, trout swim and beavers build their dams. As I took in the scene from the old US Forest Service lodge in Jackson Hole, I hoped that I would have time to paint and hike.

But I was not visiting for rest and recreation. It was August 2005, and I had been invited as governor of the Reserve Bank of New Zealand to a conference of the United States Federal Reserve.

Normally life is peaceful here, but today is all hustle and bustle. Outside the lodge, big white trucks with satellite dishes prepare to beam interviews to the world. The front door swings open before a group of muscular young men with crew-cuts and security wires plugged into their ears. In their midst is a much older man in his late seventies, short and balding with owlish glasses. Holiday-makers stop and respectfully move to the side, gawping. After the United States president, this is probably the most powerful man in the world: Alan Greenspan, chairman of the Board of Governors of the mighty Federal Reserve System of the United States.

He is here to address the annual Jackson Hole symposium of the Federal Reserve, an event at which 150 central bankers, economists and commentators discuss the world economy. In the mornings there are serious presentations; later, conference participants may go hiking. On

1

the mountain trails one hears the direct views of people with their fingers on the world's economic pulse. In the evenings they barbeque on the terrace and the economic discussions continue.

This is not just another event for Alan Greenspan. He is shortly to retire after an unprecedented eighteen years heading the most powerful economic body in the world. In his honour, the conference is entitled 'The Greenspan Era'. The great man himself opens proceedings. He gives a masterly exposition, loaded with detail and statistics, as is his style, on how the American economy has evolved since the 1960s. He describes how financial markets and monetary policy have become more sophisticated, helping economies to become more stable while countries enjoy the fruits of globalisation and innovation.

As Greenspan sits down, the journalists dash out of the room to file their copy, transmitted by satellite to the world's media and thence to the financial markets, waiting to translate his every wink and nod into market prices. Later in the morning Greenspan unexpectedly stands to ask a question; the journalists rush out to file his question as well. Other speakers give presentations, all admiring of the chairman. Their views are summarised by the lead paper from two eminent Princeton University monetary economists, Alan Blinder and Ricardo Reis: 'While there are some negatives in the record, when the score is toted up, we think he has a legitimate claim to being the greatest central banker who ever lived.'[*]

Of course, there have always been sceptics. Only two years previously, at the same conference, American academics James Stock and Mark Watson had reported on their investigation into the causes of the higher growth and more stable conditions in world economies over the past decade. In a detailed econometric study, Stock and Watson documented a number of drivers of growth but, to the general surprise of economists, they had been unable to attribute much of the new growth and stability to improved monetary policy.[†]

---

[*] Alan S. Binder and Ricardo Reis, 'Understanding the Greenspan Standard', September 2005, Princeton University, CEPS Working Paper no. 114.
[†] J. H. Stock and M. W. Watson, 'Has the Business Cycle Changed? Evidence and Explanations', August 2003, Jackson Hole symposium, Federal Reserve Bank of Kansas City.

This line of argument was well known to the experienced participants. The real insight of the 2005 conference came from another quarter. One of the new breed of financial economists, University of Chicago academic Raghuram Rajan, gave a paper entitled 'Has Financial Development Made the World Riskier?'* In a word, his answer was yes. Using data from financial instruments, he told a different story to Greenspan's, a story of rapidly changing financial markets with perverse incentives to mismanage risk and a real chance of major problems ahead. This generated a lot of argument and counter-argument.

To conclude the conference, Greenspan returned to the stand, and this time looked forward. He was more sanguine than Rajan, saying that despite ongoing challenges the current housing boom would inevitably simmer down, savings would start to improve and current account deficits would rebalance. These were reassuring words from someone who had been at the heart of the US economy for decades.

Greenspan had become chairman of the Federal Reserve Board in 1987. This date marked the start of a new growth era in the world economy, the beginning of the largest accumulation of wealth in history. With globalisation, new markets were opening up, dramatically increasing the global labour force; the Uruguay Round gave birth to the World Trade Organization, and both were encouraging developed countries to reduce their trade protection; financial markets – that network of traders, economists, bankers and fund managers – were becoming deeper and more sophisticated; and consumers worldwide were getting access to new and cheaper goods.

This all resulted in stability for the Western world. For emerging economies, however, the decade was volatile: Russian, Mexican and Brazilian debt crises echoed around the financial markets. In July 1997 the stock market in Thailand fell precipitously, sparking what became known as the East Asian Financial Crisis.

* Raghuram Rajan, 'Has Financial Development Made the World Riskier?', August 2005, Jackson Hole symposium, Federal Reserve Bank of Kansas City.

International Monetary Fund (IMF) rescue missions to countries such as Indonesia and Thailand recommended tough reforms, including better governance of banks and state enterprises, more open capital markets, freely floating exchange rates and removal of state industry protection and support schemes. But East Asian governments did not much appreciate the lectures they received from international financial institutions and the United States, and they responded in their own fashion, strengthening capital controls, continuing with fixed under-valued exchange rates to stimulate their exports and building up private and official savings as insulation from the next world shock. Initially this combination of protective policies seemed to work. When their solution also resulted in cheap goods and cheap money for the markets of the West, the latter were more inclined to approve. However, some of these policies were to brew later problems in turn.

China led the recovery with strong exporting. The world was now seeing the biggest growth in incomes ever – a typical Chinese worker born in the early 1970s while Mao Tse-tung was still alive was to see his or her income grow by up to five or six times. Unsure about the future, the Chinese population saved strongly. The Chinese Government kept interest rates low and encouraged state banks to lend freely to government and private business ventures. Some of these investments proved to be bad decisions but others were spectacularly successful.

We were seeing the birth of a second industrial revolution and, like the first, it would have far-reaching global implications. Thousands of factories were built, initially along the Chinese coastal plains and then further inland, up river valleys and in cities. Factory owners gained access to cheap capital for set-up costs, then employed cut-price labour from the huge surplus of rural farm workers who were prepared to move, work, save and remit at levels never before seen anywhere in the world. These factories imported components and materials, largely from other higher income East Asian producers, and transformed them into a wide range of industrial and consumer products, based on Western designs, for Western markets. In a short space of time this manufacturing grew in sophistication and scale of production; and the product range widened and improved in quality. Now Chinese plants could compete with other electronics manufacturers in the East and some of the primary processors of Australasia. Manufacturers in the United States found it difficult to compete, as did those in Europe who were similarly assailed by cheap manufacturing imports from the newly opened Eastern European markets.

This industrial revolution provided consumers in the West with a bonanza of products and designs at tantalising prices. Central banks around the world applauded: emerging market exports were so cheap that they helped reduce consumer prices in the West. Many countries were enjoying significant growth without generating inflation. This period became known as the 'Great Moderation', referring to the perceived end to major price and output volatility from the mid-1980s. (The term, coined by a Harvard economist James Stock in 2002, was later popularised by Ben Bernanke.) Proponents argued that the phenomenon not only represented a global shift in productivity as it raised growth in the emerging countries, but it also lifted potential growth in the West as better-off consumers could increase production without overheating their domestic economies.

Not everyone was sanguine about this. A couple of well-known central bankers expressed their doubts to me. The gist of their concern was that financial markets were too dependent on the ability of central banks to keep inflation low while growth was so high. It suited these markets to see central bankers as more powerful than we really were. One day they would learn otherwise.

As New Zealand pulled out of the East Asian crisis in 1998, we too saw good times ahead. Initially it looked like the crisis could be very damaging for New Zealand. We were not well positioned: because of rising inflation, Don Brash, in his capacity as governor of the Reserve Bank, had had to increase interest rates just prior to the crash. Our growth prospects took a hit.

But business cycles are the meat and potatoes of economists. As a student in the 1970s I had seen the effects of New Zealand's refusal to face the facts of a world where our markets were not guaranteed, the OPEC oil

5

shocks, and the excesses of the Think Big energy projects. In the late 1980s, when I was director of the New Zealand Institute of Economic Research, I saw the effects of Rogernomics when the Labour Government forced changes on a resistant economy, causing businesses to collapse, exorbitant interest rates and high unemployment. We also suffered the 1987 share market and subsequent commercial property crash. In the 1990s, as chairman of the New Zealand Commerce Commission, I oversaw some change in the dairy, aviation, forestry and other industries, and we were also trying to bed down proper business practices, getting businesses to compete in the interests of New Zealand consumers.

I was appointed secretary to the New Zealand Treasury in late 1997 at the time the East Asian crisis knocked us into recession, but the 1980s reforms had made the economy more flexible and we bounced back quickly. It seemed that at last we might be on a more vigorous growth track. We suffered unnecessary angst over the Year 2000 (Y2K) problem and the severe acute respiratory syndrome (SARS) epidemic of 2003 had little effect on the economy. Though the US tech wreck of 2000 was nasty and the events of 9/11 shocking, their economic impacts proved limited. More importantly, we were seeing improved terms of trade because of higher prices for commodities, still the backbone of the New Zealand economy. When that happens, New Zealand grows.

From 1998 to 2002, I inhabited the secretary's office in the Treasury building at number 1, The Terrace, Wellington. On the top floor, the wood-panelled office had a sweeping view of the Wellington Harbour on one side and the Beehive against the brooding Tinakori Hills on the other. There we worked at Treasury's ongoing job: keeping the quality of government spending as high as possible and trying to create the best conditions for New Zealand business to grow the economy.

When the new Labour Government entered office in 1999, they wanted more attention to social programmes, but they knew that, to finance them, they needed decent economic growth. Prime Minister Helen Clark questioned me about how we perceived the potential for expansion. She needed to know how fast the New Zealand economy could grow without overheating. Were any of our policies holding us back? Was the Reserve Bank, across the road, with its predominant

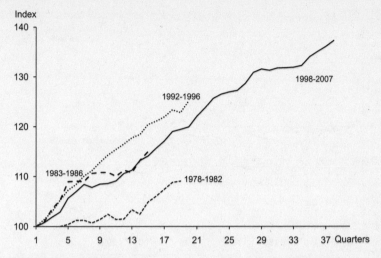

New Zealand enjoys the longest period of growth since the 1950s. The graph shows growth cycles over the last thirty years and illustrates 37 quarters of GDP growth during the 'Great Moderation'.

focus on price stability, too conservative in its view and inhibiting the economy from reaching its potential? Were there other changes our small economy should be making? We New Zealanders have a tendency to self-criticise, although at that time our growth record was actually quite impressive. Through the period from 1991 to 2002 we grew at over 4 per cent per annum, faster than Australia at the same time. But New Zealanders were spending more than they earned, and by 2002 there were signs that inflation was building again.

On 26 April 2002, I received an unexpected early-morning phone call from Don Brash, governor of the New Zealand Reserve Bank, telling me he was about to move on. With a general election approaching later that year, he was making a dramatic career change. He was to join the National Party, with a guaranteed seat in the House of Representatives. That meant he would leave the Reserve Bank immediately – in fact that very day. The financial markets were taken aback, buzzing with rumour and gossip. I too was surprised.

I did not then realise that I was about to get a much closer look at the workings of the New Zealand economy.

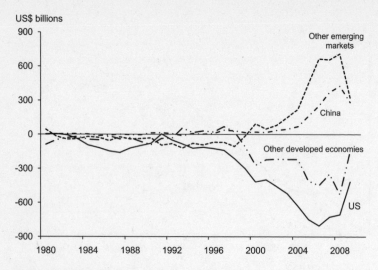

US$ billions

Other emerging markets

China

Other developed economies

US

Fast-growing global imbalances: the graph measures the growing current account imbalances by different country groupings.

After the turbulent 1990s, the 2000s seemed to be offering the world a chance to get the growth environment right at last. Strong economies in the East produced for the consumers of the West. Did it matter that some exporting nations were starting to build up large surpluses while some Western countries were recording big trade deficits? Apparently not, because global financial markets now had more sophisticated ways to finance this difference. As the global trade deficits swelled they were matched by bigger flows of global finance than the world had ever seen.

There were a number of key drivers. In the United States, President George W. Bush cut taxes, which had an immediate stimulative effect as Americans consumed more goods, an increasing proportion of them imported. US businesses experienced growth and employment was strong, but what Alan Greenspan had identified as the 'productivity miracle' of the late 1990s was fading. With reduced tax revenue, the US Government, which had achieved a fiscal surplus under President Clinton, relapsed into deficit. The US pattern of consumption-led growth was mirrored in other Western countries – in Europe, Eastern Bloc countries began exporting to the consumers of the European Union.

Economists worried about how the huge deficits of the Western countries could be sustained. In 2005, Ben Bernanke, at that time a Federal Reserve Committee member, gave an influential speech about what he described as a 'savings glut' in the East, arguing that countries such as China had their own imbalance problems, with too much household saving and too few high-return investment opportunities. As a consequence, the Eastern funding was flooding world markets, looking for returns. By implication, capital was too cheap, and this distorted consumer choices in the United States, exchange rates in Australasia and government expenditure in Western Europe.

Not only the Chinese and other big-saving East Asian countries contributed to the glut; increasingly, so did the oil-exporting nations of the Middle East and former Soviet Union. As the price of oil rose, they built big surpluses. Countries with such windfalls were encouraged by the IMF to set up sovereign wealth funds to manage them, and these funds soon became a powerhouse in world financial markets, with banks, hedge funds and mutual funds recycling massive capital flows each year.

Thus world financial markets were positioned between rampant consumers on one hand and savings gluts on the other. Operating in newly deregulated markets, they searched for new ways to bridge the needs of these two groups. It was a period of intense financial innovation. Northern Hemisphere business schools were turning out young graduates with impressive qualifications, combining finance theory with mathematics and advanced computer modelling to form a new discipline, financial engineering. Attracted by the prospects of huge remuneration, they flocked into the world's major investment banks, the likes of Merrill Lynch, Goldman Sachs and Lehman Brothers. They brought with them the pricing and risk-management models developed by Fischer Black and Nobel prize-winning economists Myron Scholes and Robert Merton, among others.

The investment banks encouraged the world's big lending banks to securitise the assets in their balance sheets; in other words, to bundle their loans and on-sell them to other parties, sometimes through a 'special purpose vehicle', a special legal entity designed to meet a particular need. This freed up the banks' capital so that they could keep lending to new customers. This practice was matched with another class of innovation – new derivative products, by which credit risk could be offset by linking it to other market prices that were more acceptable to the holder. Derivative products were not all the same – many different instruments were devised. In principle, regulations were in place to limit the risks from such developments. But a further innovation – off-balance-sheet 'structured investment vehicles' – helped institutions minimise the costs of these regulations.* For these complex instruments to be sold through financial markets, buyers needed to understand how much risk they were taking on, how to manage this risk and how to offset any residual uncertainties. To assist these assessments, the financial engineers devised a number of new risk measures.

Certification of risk levels for buyers came in the form of credit ratings. Financial instruments were examined by big rating agencies, such as Moody's and Standard & Poor's, who would award a rating from triple A down to junk status. Investment banks could then mix and match bundles of debt on the market to reach the necessary quality thresholds to get a triple A. Buyers of this debt might be smaller banks, fund managers or other financial institutions around the world, and they relied heavily on the credit ratings to assess the quality of the packages they were buying.

If they wanted further assurance, then the financial markets offered other ways to reduce risk. Buyers could go to a group of (mainly American) firms called the monoline bond insurance industry, from which they could buy insurance against any class of debts falling into default. New financial innovations offered even more certainty; holders could insure against credit risk from significant institutions by going to credit default swap (CDS) markets, thereby covering their bets about

---

* For a fascinating account, see Gillian Tett, *Fool's Gold: How the Bold Dream of a Small Tribe at J.P. Morgan was Corrupted by Wall Street Greed and Unleashed a Catastrophe*, Free Press, 2009.

the possible failure of corporate or sovereign debt. There seemed to be further assurance for risk-laden bankers: the so-called 'Greenspan put', a belief that the Federal Reserve could reduce downside risk by cutting interest rates.

With all these risk-management tools at their disposal, institutional investors also flocked into the 'repo', or repurchase-agreement markets, which allowed them to use financial securities as collateral for loans at a fixed interest rate, and in doing so, to gear up for new lending.

Together the financial developments made possible a new way for borrowers and lenders to do business: what became known as the 'originate and distribute' model. It appeared to offer significant advantages to both sides: borrowers could get money more efficiently and cheaply; lenders could package up the debt and sell it on; while, somewhere across the world, the ultimate holders could insure against the risk without having to know whom they were lending to. This was a world away from the old model of the village money lender who knew both his borrowers and how to ensure they would not renege on their debts.

These financial innovations were the subject of a central bankers' conference I attended in Switzerland in the summer of 2007. We gathered at a grand hotel built for nineteenth-century tourists in the beautiful town of Brunnen on the shores of Lake Lucerne. It was high summer. Swiss conservation laws forbid air conditioning and as we listened to world experts, we sweltered and dozed and looked longingly through the windows to the scene outside. Lake Lucerne shimmered before a backdrop of cliffs and the snow-covered peaks of the Swiss Alps soared above. The view had changed little since Turner painted the scene in watery pigments in 1843.

My mind was torn away from the scenery by a highly technical paper from a young American business school professor. He was telling us about a new class of financial derivatives that were smarter and more complicated than anything seen to date. With PowerPoint and whiteboard, he showed us how these derivatives were put together, how they absorbed and reallocated risk and how these residual risks could be re-engineered to reduce them even further. Then he looked around the room and asked, 'How many of you really understand that?' No response. 'How many of you understand who ultimately holds this risk?' No hands went up. 'How many of you know how this could unravel?' Again, silence. He went on, 'I think there are only a few people in the world who could understand this class of transactions. You do not employ any of them, neither do the banks, and neither do the credit rating agencies who will rate them.'

It was a sobering moment for the senior central bankers present. For the first time I confronted seriously the implications of these financial instruments and the damage they could do if they were misused. We did not then know the scale these derivatives were to reach a scant few months later – almost a quadrillion US dollars – that is, a thousand trillion, $1,000,000,000,000,000!

All these technical developments in sophisticated wholesale finance would have been pointless without a large customer base eager to borrow. By far the largest group of potential borrowers was American house buyers. Housing markets in the West had been growing since 2002. Confident Western consumers were not just consuming more, they wanted to invest more. They invested in stock markets around the world; they invested in financial instruments; but most of all they invested in property. Property investment came in many varieties – securitised property, land development, time shares, vacation accommodation at home or offshore – but overwhelmingly, Western consumers bought houses. In countries as diverse as Spain, Ireland, the United Kingdom and Australia, households borrowed as never before to buy and improve houses. The more house prices appreciated, the more demand there seemed to be for new housing assets in household balance sheets. And increasingly that housing took on the characteristics of a financial asset: intermediary financed, highly leveraged, subject to price cycles and hard to control by monetary policy.

For very particular reasons, the biggest boom in house financing took place in the United States. In the 1930s Depression, Franklin D. Roosevelt had put in place Federal assistance measures designed to stimulate the moribund economy. One of these was to set up what became known as Fannie Mae and younger sibling Freddie Mac, which are government-sponsored private institutions acting as mortgage intermediaries.* Because of their perceived implicit government guarantees, the financial markets willingly funded them. At various times in the 1970s, and again in the 1990s, US presidents, rather than curtailing these big institutions, used them to promote cheap home loans to Americans who had little or poor credit history.

The home loans industry encouraged these buyers. Mortgage brokers were given incentives to shovel mortgages out the door. Loans offered at unrealistically low teaser rates lured householders to borrow beyond their means, leading to mortgages which were later to become known as 'subprime'. The quality of these players was not always good. Economist David Hale reports that 20 per cent of all mortgage brokers in the state of Ohio had criminal records.† Funds flowed via Freddie and Fannie and, with uneven state-level regulation, huge volumes of loans were given to low-income households who were relying on unrealistic capital gains in order to keep financing their homes.

This toxic mix was made more dangerous by two additional features. One was the tradition of non-recourse loans, legal in most American states but not in many other countries. These allow a defaulting borrower to walk away from the mortgaged assets and not be pursued for the loan, thereby increasing default risk. The second feature was unusually low global interest rates. After the East Asian crisis, central banks cut cash rates rapidly to stimulate demand. Alan Greenspan at the Federal Reserve led the way, cutting rates by over 5 per cent during the turbulent year of 2000. Though his cuts that year turned out to be far-sighted, the Fed sat on the low rates for another three years before gradually increasing them – too long and too slow. Thus, for the first half of the decade, US home-buyers were taking out loans at incredibly cheap rates, and this continued even as house prices rapidly appreciated.

Did the financial markets think this was sustainable? The prevailing view, one that I heard expressed by Alan Greenspan a number of times, was that the structured finance market promoted both efficiency

---

* The name 'Fannie Mae' derives from the Federal National Mortgage Association (FNMA); and Freddie Mac from the Federal Home Mortgage Corporation (FHMC).
† David Hale, 'Jail the Bankers', *The International Economy*, Winter 2010.

(delivering funding to people who had never been able to afford it was efficient from their perspective) and stability (being so diversified that risks in one area were balanced by gains in another). The former assertion turned out to be partially correct, the latter was about to be tested.

Housing was not the only international asset to grow: commodities were also making a comeback. International oil prices had been subdued for some years, which hurt Middle Eastern producers but helped lay the foundations for stronger global growth. Indeed, some economists have argued that the period of US great moderation was not driven by domestic productivity at all, but by cheap oil. US consumers have always been significant buyers of world oil, but in the early 2000s China and other emerging manufacturers also became huge industrial buyers. By mid-decade the international oil price had doubled to the region of US$60 a barrel. Analysts speculated where this would end. Many agreed with the line taken by *The Economist*, that strong demand would eventually lead to improved exploration and refining, bringing the price back down toward the significantly lower marginal cost of 'swing' producers such as Canada.

But that did not happen. Instead, through 2007, even as the first signs of financial weakness appeared, the oil price in US dollars rose inexorably, hitting US$100 by the end of the year. Rational forecasting seemed hardly possible, and the futures market provided conflicting signals. The demand from emerging markets continued strong, but there was something more than the short-term laws of supply and demand at work. Oil had become a financial instrument. Many global funds started to buy into the futures and derivatives markets linked to oil, never taking delivery of a barrel but, rather, seeking to tie investment returns to the rise in oil prices. And prices continued to soar, even as economies choked on the increases. By mid-2008, oil had hit almost US$150, a rise of 750 per cent in a decade.

It was not just oil. Other energy prices like gas followed closely. Then, worried by oil dependence, major consuming countries set up big subsidies for agricultural producers to grow crops for bio-fuel conversion – particularly bio-ethanol from maize in the United States and bio-diesel from soy and other crops in Germany. Now the prices of

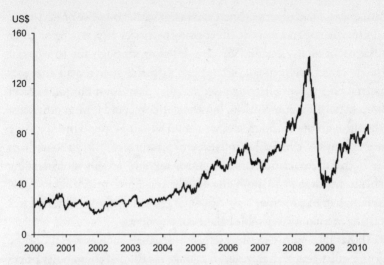

We struggled with inflation as the oil price reached US$145 – not knowing that, over the next four months, it would slump to $40 as the crisis hit. The graph measures the Dubai oil price in US$ per barrel.

grains and pulses were linked to energy, and they too became a favourite target for financial traders. In this commodities boom, precious and industrial metal prices also soared, pushed by strong emerging market demand and underwritten by adventurous financial markets.

In New Zealand, we were monitoring these events. If subprime issues, securitisation and derivatives were still far off, the oil price hikes were only too close. Arriving at work each morning, I would turn on my Reuters screen with some trepidation. The homepage has an unappealing mix of blue and red numbers and graphs. Half way down the screen, a little tab labelled 'BRENT' records the spot price in US dollars for Brent North Sea light-grade crude oil, an important industry reference. Day by day I watched its steady climb. At our daily and weekly meetings we talked about what was causing the increase in the price of oil, how high the price would go and when it would fall. Repeatedly our forecasts turned out to be too low. Several times in front of parliamentary committees, under questioning from Green Members of

Parliament, I had to retract and explain our earlier oil price projections.

Our main worry was the effect rising oil prices were having on price inflation in New Zealand. We view inflation through the lens of our Policy Targets Agreement, a contract with the government that sets specific targets for delivering price stability. It was not our job to react directly to rising pump prices, but their effects could lead to other cost rises through the economy and we would have to respond by increasing interest rates. We had other inflationary pressures to worry about. Plans for both an Auckland regional petrol tax and an emissions trading scheme threatened to push the fragile consumer price index (CPI) even higher. In addition, New Zealand's growing import bill for oil was starting to hit our vulnerable balance of payments.

Other tabs on my Reuters screen bear labels such as 'CRB' for the Commodity Research Bureau, an average measure of commodity prices around the world; 'GSCI', the Goldman Sachs commodity index; and 'GOLD'. At the touch of a button, graphs pop up. They showed that, beyond oil, price escalation was hitting many other commodities: precious metals, minerals and such heavily traded agricultural commodities as soy products.

Some of that was good news for New Zealand. Escalating aluminium prices, for example, helped exports from the Tiwai Point smelter. In early 2007 world dairy prices shot up – in international terms, they more than doubled in the course of the year. This was very good for our terms of trade, which continued its decade-long improvement, and for chief dairy exporter Fonterra, dairy farmers and the banks that rushed to lend to them. But in the game of economics, there is always another side: the dairy price put pressure on other land users, the cost of living and the New Zealand dollar, which appreciated by over 10 per cent that year, to the unhappiness of other exporters. Though the high New Zealand dollar hurt exporters, it also meant that imports became cheaper, and New Zealand consumers enjoyed a shopping bonanza. A low US dollar, cheap Asian production and some new big Australian retailers provided a heady mix; consumption rose rapidly.

The commodities boom had other interesting effects. New Zealand became a significant oil exporter for a couple of years as the high prices encouraged the developers of the Maari oil field to pump out reserves. And at the Reserve Bank we had our own windfall. In a change to our coinage, big clunky coins became lighter-weight and smaller, made of (cheaper) steel with fine alloy coatings on top. The old coins were made of copper and nickel, and these minerals were now earning record prices on world markets. For a couple of years we became scrap metal dealers, shipping off container after container of old 'silver' coins to smelters in Korea. That earned over $5 million for the New Zealand taxpayer.

The econometric models at the Reserve Bank focus on a key driver of New Zealand household confidence and consumption: house prices. When prices are strong the housing market runs hot with demand and new housing investments get under way. And when New Zealanders buy a house, they also buy fixtures, fittings and furnishings. One retailer told me he even sells more chainsaws to people with new houses – only in New Zealand! This relationship between house prices and household consumption is much closer in New Zealand than it is in other countries. As New Zealanders have few assets of other types, when house prices go up we feel wealthier and spend freely. When we can afford it, we are inclined to put more money into home improvements, holiday houses, investor housing or property funds.

Such were the volatile conditions building in the first half of the decade. House prices were rising as much as 25 per cent in a year by 2005; and consumption grew by 7 per cent in this five-year period, much faster than our incomes. The government had been saving; so had the business sector; but households had not. Despite relatively high interest rates (mortgages cost up to 10 per cent at this time), householders thought borrowing extra for housing was a good deal. Their plan was to keep a significant part of their housing assets debt-funded, withdrawing equity to boost their income. Though only a minority of New Zealand households have outstanding mortgages on their own home, the debt of those who do is significant. Credit lent into the household sector reached $2 billion per month in 2006 and, however much house prices rose, the increase was not sufficient to outweigh the growth in household debt. Households wanted to borrow and the banks were prepared to lend liberally.

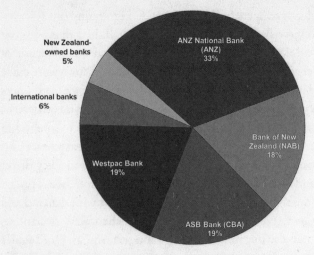

Four Australian banks dominate the New Zealand market. The pie diagram measures the share of banking assets held by the big four Australian banks in New Zealand – together with other international banks and the New Zealand-owned banks: Kiwibank, TSB Bank and SBS Bank (December 2009). Source: bank disclosure statements

Most banking operations in New Zealand are not overly complicated: they involve gaining access to international funds to feed the demand for home mortgages. The four big Australian banks have long dominated the New Zealand system – as ANZ National, ASB, BNZ and Westpac – and they watch one another closely. But this period saw a new player on the block: Kiwibank, a New Zealand government-owned bank founded in 2002 that was a subsidiary of New Zealand Post. Though very small, it marketed and lent mortgages aggressively. As the Australian banks saw their traditional New Zealand market shares under attack, they intensified their own advertising and promotion of loans. BNZ, for example, in 2004 launched an 'unbeatable' campaign, which promised to cut lending costs.

With all this in play, credit figures grew and some measures of quality (like loan to value ratios) started to deteriorate as the debt flow increased. But the banks were making good profits on this trade and kept on lending. They partly used retail deposits to fund these loans but were forced, because locals in Australia and New Zealand weren't saving much, to raise most of the money in offshore markets. Some of this was done by issuing debt in longer-term capital markets where banks received wholesale loans of several years' maturity. However, they found a significant portion in short-term money markets where they found it easy to get big loans cheaply. Typically raised in US dollars, these funds were swapped into New Zealand dollars for lending purposes, with other offshore parties taking the foreign exchange risk often via multinational issuance of New Zealand dollar investments overseas. These were the parallel transactions where the semi-mythical Belgian dentists bought eurokiwis and Japanese housewives bought eurodashi bonds. For years, New Zealand home loan borrowers, Australian lending banks, Wall Street financiers and East Asian savers formed a symbiotic relationship.

At the Reserve Bank we regulate the banks for prudential soundness, so we watched the build-up of housing debt with some concern. When an IMF-led taskforce, the Financial Sector Assessment Program, audited our system in 2003, we performed stress tests on our banks to see what would happen to their balance sheets if conditions worsened and lending went sour. We tried an experiment, assessing the effects of a bad recession with unemployment rocketing to 9 per cent, property prices dropping 20 per cent and incomes falling too. The results of that and other nasty scenarios were encouraging from the viewpoint of system stability: though bank profits would be hurt, their balance sheets would still be sound.

However, confidence in the system was not the only issue. New Zealand was building a large private debt, much of it related to borrowing for houses. Letting banks make these decisions for us was not always in our national interest. In early 2007 we started talking to them about moderating their lending. To my surprise, several bankers readily agreed that things had got too loose. We obtained assurances that those responsible for the most aggressive promotion of loans – who were most in danger from the falling quality standards – would reform their practices.

At the same time we faced another challenge. Banking practices differ around the world, but we ensure ours meet international standards.

These are set by a somewhat shadowy group called the Basel Committee on Banking Supervision. Comprised of representatives of larger countries (not including New Zealand), the group meets in Switzerland at the Bank for International Settlements (BIS). Over the decade they had been developing a new set of banking standards known as Basel II. These recommended regulatory capital requirements more closely based on the risk of lending. House lending was rated as particularly low risk, so the local banks argued vigorously that this justified them actually increasing their housing loans off the same capital base. Our concern was that though rocketing household debt might not bring down a bank, the economy could not cope with with such high levels. The data looked acute: from 2000 to 2004 house prices rose 50 per cent, and lending was still growing more strongly than people's incomes. We were running down our savings and doing so at an increasing rate. When the Organisation for Economic Co-operation and Development (OECD) declined to publish our official savings figures because they looked unreliably low, it was a wake-up call. Although these figures did not fully take into account all offshore saving by New Zealanders and the tendency for households to save through trusts, we had no doubt about the trend: things were getting worse.

Government savings could not make up for New Zealanders' inclination to borrow and the external debt was starting to mount. Our balance of payments offered little good news. The country's trade in goods and services was slightly in deficit, but we were more worried that the investment income balance (the amount companies take out of New Zealand, less our earnings abroad) was seriously in deficit. In 2006 our current account deficit reached 9 per cent of gross domestic product (GDP), a level at which alarm bells often sound in financial markets. Surprisingly, there was little reaction. Foreign and capital exchange markets continued to fund the New Zealand dollar strongly. Visiting credit rating agencies listened to our stories about strong growth, discounted our fears about emerging imbalance and left our ratings intact. Delegations from the Paris-based OECD and the Washington-based IMF visited each year, and together we scratched our heads about the buoyant markets and the fragile situation.

I aired some of these concerns in a speech to the Wellington Chamber of Commerce in March 2007. After sitting through an unhealthy breakfast, I addressed the gathering of business people on the subject of 'easy money' and what it meant for New Zealand. The message was cautionary. Booming world liquidity meant more and more funds were available for housing, which put pressure on interest rates; while the carry trade – in which traders borrow funds in low-yielding currencies and flock to currencies with big yields – exacerbated the strong exchange rate. All this created problems for a small open economy trying to run its own monetary policy. The problem is not unique to New Zealand. I had talked to counterparts in countries as far off and different as South Africa, Hungary and Iceland who were all suffering from the same situation. (Even Greenspan's successor, Ben Bernanke, at this time was complaining that the mighty Federal Reserve was having trouble influencing interest rates through monetary policy!)

Through this period we had been increasing the official cash rate (OCR), the Reserve Bank's main tool for influencing short-term commercial lending rates. The years 2004 and 2005 were tough as, with hard decisions and a lot of angst, we had to push up the OCR nine times to try and slow a dangerously heated economy. As usual in such times, we encountered criticism from analysts, journalists, business people and politicians who railed against us for slowing growth. But headline inflation was rising inextricably and, pushed by oil prices, was heading beyond the 1–3 per cent zone that the Policy Targets Agreement specifies for medium-term inflation. After holding rates for a year and seeing no relief from the pressures of the housing market, we pushed the OCR up to a record 8.25 per cent in July 2007. But as we had always known, a rate this high attracts foreign funds, forcing the dollar up even further. It was good news for New Zealand borrowers seeking cheap credit but made life tougher for exporters being paid in US dollars.

Floods of emails came my way around this time about inflation and particularly about the strong dollar. Some of the messages were understanding, some were thoughtful and some abusive. At the same time my assistant, Sandy Anderson, was taking rough phone calls from angry New Zealanders. We were also getting harsh media treatment saying we should have increased rates earlier. We had done this but, ironically, many of the commentators had opposed the earlier increases. For a couple of the most irritating, I took a vicarious pleasure in confronting them with their previous statements.

I also received a death threat. Unlike most of my overseas colleagues, I lead a relatively easy life, unencumbered by security guards. I walk to work and I walk home. Once a press photographer had ambushed me from behind a bush on my way to work, but that was the worst that had ever happened. Now on my way home after the death threat, climbing up through the Botanic Garden in the dark (it was winter, there had been a power failure and all the lights were out) I wondered whether I was being sensible walking alone. Was my would-be assailant an unhappy bankrupt letting off steam or a deranged person who might be a real threat? Economic pressure can have unexpected consequences, and some people out there were hurting.

CHAPTER 2

Gathering Storm Clouds
2007–August 2008

On a fine spring day in 2002, a little windy as it sometimes can be in Wellington, I had been walking along the waterfront to an appointment when my cellphone rang. It was Bill Wilson, chairman of the non-executive directors of the Reserve Bank. Would I accept appointment as the new governor of the Reserve Bank?

I would be moving only 50 metres across the street, from the New Zealand Treasury to the Bank building at number 2, The Terrace. But it was a very different job, with a very different set of responsibilities. What would it involve? The role of the Reserve Bank is a crucial one, helping to stabilise the economy and the banking system. I would have management autonomy, but would be held accountable by the Board – with a single monetary policy decision-maker, it is pretty clear whom to hold responsible.

I inherited from Dr Don Brash, my predecessor, an exceptionally small and focused operation, trimmed by the efficiency measures of the 1990s (the total staff in June 2002 numbered only 185) but still covering the wide range of expertise required of a 'full-service' central bank. The government had resisted the overseas trend of splitting the financial regulator from the central bank, and the bank also provided cash, carried out monetary policy, operated payment systems and managed liquidity and foreign reserves. A pioneer in modern central banking, Dr Brash had found innovative ways to re-engineer many of these operations.

The New Zealand Reserve Bank was arguably the smallest serious central bank in the world. Much bigger countries such as France and Germany, which had delegated monetary policy and currency to the regional European Central Bank, still had over 10,000 employees at their central banks. We frequently host visitors from other central banks who are eager to learn from the New Zealand model. They wonder, for example, how on earth we meet New Zealand's currency needs (primarily supplying banknotes and coins and monitoring their quality) with a team of only a dozen people. The answer: super-efficient systems, extensive outsourcing and an increased role for commercial banks.

Management of the Reserve Bank in untroubled times is reasonably straightforward. It helps that the organisation is all in one building in central Wellington, staffed by skilled people who know their tasks and have delegated powers. I have a great team of managers with a mix of expertise and experience. As we took on some extra responsibilities from 2007, we built up staff numbers a little, but 'small but perfectly formed' remained our unspoken motto. In addition, we worked on staff culture, encouraging people to learn from one another. There are few central banks where an economic forecaster can walk down a few flights of stairs to talk to the man in charge of regulating our biggest banks, the woman running the wholesale electronic payments in the banking system, the staff who monitor the overnight domestic markets, the traders managing the foreign reserves or the person who controls the delivery of new notes and coins. We needed to exploit these connections.

One critical area that was still developing in 2002 was bank supervision. In the past the Reserve Bank had managed to get by with a light-handed approach to this, but the banks were getting bigger, their balance sheets more complex and finance companies (we call them 'non-banks') more risky. To supervise banks you need people at a senior level with experience in financial markets and in commercial banks, who know how decisions are made, how markets work, how banks operate – and what happens when things go wrong. The Reserve Bank Board had taken a calculated risk in approaching me: I had never worked in a central bank or a trading bank before. A priority for me was to appoint deputies who were highly experienced. An early deputy, Adrian Orr, began to lift our capability as a bank regulator, until he was promoted to chief executive at the New Zealand Superannuation Fund. My new deputy, Grant Spencer, began his career at the Reserve Bank then worked for a major Australian bank for a decade. His expertise is in being able to see the big picture. Assistant Governor Dr Don Abel has spent a long career mainly in a New Zealand bank, and he brings a deep knowledge of operations in these complex organisations. The other assistant governor, Dr John McDermott, is a younger man who had a distinguished career in the IMF, banks and academia before returning to the Reserve Bank a few years ago.

The Reserve Bank Act says one of our tasks is to 'promote soundness and efficiency in the financial system'. We want to make sure banks are well governed, that they obey New Zealand law, pay New Zealand taxes and support the New Zealand financial system. The four main banks are owned by Australians, but they have to fit our regulatory conditions. We require them to carry adequate capital, to meet our governance standards, to be incorporated locally, to maintain appropriate local capability and to have risk management and crisis plans in place. It would be hard for a country the size of New Zealand to have its own large banks. Instead, we have been a world leader in developing regulatory standards for banks, what the international community calls 'host regulations'.

As international banking grew more complex, we started revising banking standards from the early 2000s, strengthening policies such as offshoring conditions, our requirements for banks moving functions to Australia or elsewhere to retain the ability to carry out core local banking in a crisis. In addition, we required large banks to incorporate in New Zealand. This alarmed the Australian banks, who were not backward in making their concerns felt. We went to the New Zealand Bankers' Association to hear their arguments, only to be told that they would not be expressing a view: instead we would hear from the Australian Bankers' Association. And we certainly did. As the Australian lobbying machine kicked into gear, we received dozens of telephone calls and letters (mainly helpful, but some legalistic) from the banks. Next, Australian Treasurer Peter Costello was on the phone to the New Zealand Minister of Finance, Michael Cullen, giving him his views about what we ought to do.

The Australian response to our proposals was to call New Zealanders 'honorary Aussies' and include us under the (internationally unusual) Australian depositor preference regime. That means that if one of the Australian banks fails and it ends up in liquidation, Australian depositors have first preference over other creditors. Our concern was that we would lose control of New Zealand incorporated banks in a crisis, as bank resolutions would be carried out by Australian administrators under Australian law, with disputes being heard in Australian courts. Not only might New Zealand lenders and depositors lose their property rights, it could also cost New Zealand taxpayers: if an Australian bank failed, there could be a deal done in Canberra back-rooms, then the Australian Government could send New Zealand taxpayers a bill for our share of the cost. This did not fit our approach to dealing with failed banks – since the early 2000s we had been developing a more structured set of options, outlined in our weighty *Crisis Resolution Handbook*. In addition, it would be hard to ensure a competitive playing field in New Zealand, and even harder to insist on a proper tax take for the government.

The disagreement came to a head at the second Australia New Zealand Leadership Forum in Melbourne in April 2005. These meetings are an opportunity for government, business and academic leaders from the two countries to get together and look at ways to bring the two countries closer. The Australian political race to succeed John Howard was then in full swing and it had been a rugged couple of days in Australian politics. When Peter Costello addressed the New Zealand–Australian meeting he was in no mood to be trifled with. At the rostrum he cast aside his prepared speech and spoke off the cuff. In essence, he said, 'You guys in New Zealand have to get real. If you want to be part of a single economic market with us you can forget having your own banking system. Remember, you sold your banks to us: you don't own your financial system any more. Leave the regulation to us.' He didn't beat about the bush. In our view, this was a misinterpretation: true, we had allowed foreign ownership of our banks, but this did not mean giving away our 'financial system', that combination of institutions, markets, funding, regulations and banking that allows transactions to take place. It is tremendously important that New Zealand be able to control its own financial system in order to survive a crisis. We often have interests in common with Australia – but there are times when they diverge. In my response, I objected strongly to Costello's argument. It was a tough meeting, but a groundswell of New Zealand views in the room backed me up.

Until then, Minister Michael Cullen had not particularly disputed Treasurer Costello's views that Australian regulators could do the job for us. He had not seen a New Zealand financial system in real crisis, and perhaps thought we were exaggerating the risks. He and I discussed the matter over the following weeks, and I also talked to the banks. One prominent bank asserted that we were worrying unnecessarily about a bank failure, which they claimed was a one-in-a-thousand-year event. We took a more conservative view of the risk probabilities, and so did our colleagues in Treasury. I believe Dr Cullen came to agree.

At this stage we saw the Reserve Bank of New Zealand as a sort of home guard or peacetime army that, in the event of a crisis, would protect both the New Zealand financial system (which in turn would help stabilise the New Zealand economy) and the interests of New Zealanders. We proceeded to strengthen big bank regulation with tighter requirements for Board membership. We also required banks to put in place procedures to handle stress and resolve problems in a crisis. These measures were completed just in time: in the following years we were all to be tested.

The year 2007 was a strange one for many central banks: rising financial worries did not seem to be reflected in the real economy which continued strong. In New Zealand our growth track had begun to moderate and inflation had come off its peaks. We thought we had successfully contained housing market buoyancy but, here and elsewhere, exuberance bubbled over again, this time with prices jumping in the oil market, shortly to be followed by other commodities and assets. We had raised our official cash rate to 7.25 per cent, and that encouraged carry traders to invest in the New Zealand dollar, pushing our exchange rate higher and squeezing exporters. As we still saw spending on New Zealand housing and other signs of an overheated economy, we realised reluctantly we would have to tighten interest rates further. Up went the OCR again, four times through the year, hitting a new high of 8.25 per cent in July and starting at last to really bite.

At the same time we used our new policies to intervene in the foreign exchange markets. We had long been ambivalent about this. One reason that we held reserves was to help a falling New Zealand dollar in a major crisis – if our foreign exchange market were at risk of jamming up altogether, the Reserve Bank of New Zealand would need to be able to support the market for our currency by continuing to transact while others were staying on the sidelines. But this was the opposite problem: a New Zealand dollar valued at around US80 cents was too high for New Zealand exporters to tolerate. Our new policy was to intervene selectively – to sell the New Zealand dollar at a peak and buy it back in a trough in order to moderate the most extreme currency fluctuations, influence the markets and knock the top off the currency at its height. The tactic aroused huge media interest, financial market comment and some controversy. Our own expectations were far more limited than those of so-called experts. We used a mixture of overt and covert operations to buy US dollars in the market and to ensure buyers of New Zealand currency remained uncertain about just how many New Zealand dollars we were selling through this period.

The interventions went more or less as we had hoped, and gradually the pressure on the New Zealand dollar lifted, making exporters more competitive. The disadvantage of our interventions was that the Reserve Bank would now hold an 'open' FX position. That meant that part of its balance sheet would be held in US not New Zealand dollars and, as the exchange rate moved, so we would gain or lose money. We were soon to learn how this would complicate our balance sheet.

Finance companies also started to show signs of stress that year. Some New Zealand finance companies are long established and conservative, lending on consumer finance and industrial equipment, but there had been huge growth in finance companies operating in the property development sector. As lending conditions worsened, many of these firms proved very fragile. We had given speeches and written articles over the previous few years, warning investors, often older people, to be wary of the risks of investing in the finance companies claiming to offer very high returns. It gave us no pleasure at all to be proved right.

At the end of 2006 and in early 2007, we started to hear about property finance companies in trouble. Most were very small, and as individual failures they did not greatly concern us. But in the second half of the 2007, bigger finance companies started to fall like flies. As each one entered into liquidation, receivership or moratorium, media speculation turned to the next. We saw angry scenes of elderly debenture holders haranguing hapless managers at meetings. The pattern seemed clear: poor governance, spider-web company structures, vulnerable business models, mismatched balance sheets, bad management and inadequate supervision by the trustee companies.

At the Reserve Bank we started to worry: were the combined failures big enough to lead to a deposit run on the banks? The answer seemed to be no, in fact the banks were benefitting from a flight to quality. Did the failures point to fragile business models and practices in the banks themselves? Again, we thought not, the banks being much more sophisticated organisations than many finance companies. However, news of New Zealand finance company failures, despite their small size, was starting to spread overseas. I was repeatedly questioned about them during international financial market presentations and the Australian media began to highlight them. Now property development companies started to complain they could not gain access to second-tier finance to top up existing funds, and some big developments began to dry up.

The government recognised that this part of the financial system had not been properly regulated in the past. After a lot of policy work and political thinking in 2007, Cabinet decided that the responsibility for regulation should move to the Reserve Bank. We would now regulate the non-banks – finance companies (all sorts), building societies (mainly small and cautious organisations) and credit unions (tiny). It seemed a sensible move, but I was under no illusions: looking after this very heterogeneous industry could be very tricky.

I was even more wary of the government's next step, which was to assign the responsibility for regulation of insurance companies to the Reserve Bank. Insurance risk is a very different concept from banking risk, and one where we had no particular experience. And I did not want to turn the Reserve Bank into a large, heavy-handed mega-regulator, having seen the results of that in other countries.

More worrying were moves to regulate anti-money laundering and counter-terrorist financing. New Zealand had no record of problems in these areas but, since the events of 9/11, there had been strong international pressure for all countries to meet the same standards as those in problem regions. We fielded a number of fraught phone calls at unsociable times of day and night from a US administration determined that other countries converge on their standard. New Zealand had little choice, and legislation was passed. Now we had another job on our hands – ensuring financial institutions were not open to suspicious transactions.

As it turned out, the first signs we saw of international financial calamity had nothing to do with money laundering or terrorist financing. The trigger was subprime lending. These low-quality United States mortgages that had been packaged and re-packaged several times now quietly lay festering in financial balance sheets around the world.

In April 2007, a medium-sized US financial firm called New Century Financial filed in court for Chapter 11 bankruptcy. Such filings happen all the time, and this one did not attract much interest. Federal Reserve Chairman Ben Bernanke told the US Congress that the failure 'does not appear to have spilled over to a significant extent'.

I would like to say that in New Zealand we all recognised the importance of this bankruptcy at the time, but I cannot. Indeed, I had never heard of the symbolically named 'New Century'. In my case, it was not until 9 August, when one of the giant French banks, BNP Paribas, froze two funds consisting of subprime assets citing 'complete evaporation of liquidity in the market', that I really became aware of what was happening. I will even admit to googling 'subprime mortgages' to learn more about these toxic assets.

Indeed, it would have been hard to miss the BNP Paribas announcement, because it caused major jitters in world markets. Very soon the nervousness reached New Zealand. We saw cash surplus banks holding on to money overnight rather than lending it short term to other banks, the usual practice. This caused shortages for the deficit banks, and rumours started to spread through the market. After observing this volatility for a few days, we thought it wise to issue a public statement that we were closely following international financial developments and that we would ensure that the domestic markets would have enough cash to function satisfactorily. This relieved some of the nervousness but cash shortages persisted, so a week later we announced that we would broaden the security we require of banks borrowing from us in the overnight markets – in addition to government securities, we would now accept bills from New Zealand banks (other than the borrower) as adequate security. This further soothed the jitters.

As the flurry of markdowns on subprime instruments continued around North America and Europe, we wanted to ensure that we didn't have a problem with low-quality mortgages in New Zealand. The quality of New Zealand bank lending had eroded slightly in 2006, but we had identified that problem, and, by early 2007, banks were tightening the standards on their higher loan-to-value transactions.

Did the Australasian banks hold any of the US-originated subprime mortgages? It took a while before we could be sure of the answer. It emerged that in New Zealand they held hardly any. But in Australia, two banks had to declare holdings of US mortgage products which had lost value heavily. Fortunately these holdings were small relative to their total balance sheets. Finally, were the Australian banks exposed to banks that were themselves exposed to subprime risks? We hoped this would not become a problem as we watched the crisis unfold in the Northern Hemisphere.

A month later, things worsened noticeably: Northern Rock hit the headlines. Not as some people thought, a Newcastle rock group, Northern Rock had been a successful British building society that had gained a banking licence and grown very fast, lending mortgages to British homeowners. Praised by industry commentators for its innovation, it relied heavily for funding not on retail depositors like traditional banks, but on short-term wholesale credit. But the new nervousness in the markets brought a sudden credit crunch, and Northern Rock could not refinance fast enough. On 13 September the BBC revealed that Northern Rock had been granted emergency lending support from the Bank of England, using its lender-of-last resort powers. The effect on the British public was electric: immediately the Bank's electronic website was deluged with withdrawal requests. It soon crashed. The next day depositors formed queues in the high streets, withdrawing £2 billion. This was the biggest run on a British bank for over a century. It was arrested only after a number of promises by the British Government to guarantee savings; eventually the crippled bank had to be nationalised. To all around the world, this was a salutary reminder that old-fashioned bank runs can still happen.

For some time now my wife, Jenny Morel, and I had been planning a holiday. Jenny runs a venture capital fund. Her investments in a stable of small, New Zealand-originated high technology firms are always stressful, and her work was not made any easier by the turbulent world financial markets. I had been feeling the pressures of late-night phone calls and early-morning market shocks. When friends Cathy and Steve Franks invited us on a walking tour of archaeological sites in Western Turkey, we jumped at the opportunity. I did have a niggling worry about the current vulnerabilities, but Deputy Governor Grant Spencer took over my Reserve Bank duties, and with my BlackBerry I could stay in touch, even in remote locations. So we packed our bags, boots and hiking poles, and were off.

Walking the sites of early Hellenic civilisation, exploring the Roman buildings of Ephesus and painting the delicate beauty of an Aegean morning proved a great tonic. Our only disaster was not financial: I was sitting on the roof of our small hotel in Istanbul sketching the panorama of minarets, palaces and the distant straits of Marmara, when Steve came on to the terrace, laptop in hand, face long – the All Blacks had lost their World Cup rugby game against France!

Although perhaps some thought so, the worsening trends in the New Zealand economy were not just due to post-World Cup gloom. By the time I returned home, it was becoming clear that the subprime crisis was not going to blow away. I was reminded of the remark attributed to investor Warren Buffett: 'Derivatives are like sex. It's not who *we're* sleeping with, it's who *they're* sleeping with that's the problem.' A string of disturbing financial results was starting to emerge from the big international banks. In October UBS, the giant Swiss bank, announced US$3.4 billion in losses, mainly from subprime investments. That both chairman and chief executive stepped down underlined the gravity. At the same time, the world's biggest bank, New York's Citigroup, revealed a loss of $3.1 billion; only a fortnight later it had to increase the write-down to $9 billion. It needed more capital and needed it urgently. A month later the Abu Dhabi Investment Authority came up with US$7.5 billion in extra funding, but the wounds had not been cauterised and within months these losses reeked of gangrene. At the end of October, Wall Street investment bank Merrill Lynch announced a nearly $8 billion loss on bad debts, and the chief executive offered his resignation.

Faced with these mounting problems in major banks, US Treasury Secretary Henry Paulson was working desperately behind the scenes. He announced a private sector alliance of banks to try and prevent further mortgage defaults. But the days of US regulators arranging clubby backroom deals among banks – last used successfully with Long-Term Capital Management during the hedge fund crisis of the mid-1990s – were now numbered. Other banks healthy enough to help with a rescue were few and far between.

Could monetary policy help? In September 2007 the Federal Reserve decided it needed to start cutting the target Federal funds rate. They cut again in October, and by December 100 basis points had been slashed off the rate, a far swifter drop than in a normal downturn. In early December, President George W. Bush, who had so far maintained his distance from the crisis (arguing it was a job for the experts), announced plans to help more than one million US homeowners facing foreclosure.

You can cut rates, but that doesn't mean the banks will lend. Recognising that, on 12 December the Federal Reserve announced its Term Auction Facility: they would auction term credit to the banks to keep funds circulating in the system. In an unusual example of international cooperation, five leading central banks around the world offered billions of dollars to the banking system, and swap lines were agreed with the Fed to help provide scarce US-dollar funding outside the States. As we watched the international scene, trying to assess the turmoil, international banks would ring us with predictions of further gloom. I recall in particular a depressing late-night call from the chairman and deputy chairman of a giant international bank with whom we had longstanding relationships. The two had been around the world's financial markets for decades, and they thought this was going to be the worst crisis of their careers. I discussed the call the next day with our head of financial markets at the Reserve Bank. We both felt the bankers were being too pessimistic.

The picture for New Zealand and Australia did not look so serious at this stage. The northern financial markets were urgently trying to identify holders of toxic subprime assets. They concluded that most of these were held in North America and Europe. To them, Australasia seemed toxin free, with transparent forms of bank lending and funding. Consequently the Australasian banks were not overly penalised in offshore markets and funding continued to flow.

The end of the year can be tense for financial markets, even in good times. Traders are squaring up their positions; their accountants are reporting quarter-end results. Though less business takes place, sometimes a group of traders will try and take advantage of these thinner markets to move prices and exploit the situation. The international financial markets remain open through the Christmas and new year period. At the Reserve Bank we have to be vigilant about unexpected developments and alert to any possible liquidity blockages. We arranged meticulous phone and email call-trees among staff and discussed tactics before we went on Christmas break.

My wife and I own a small forestry block in the foothills of the Tararua Range, an hour and a half north of Wellington. We welcomed home our two sons from study in the United States, and headed for the hills. There we have a rustic New Zealand-style bach on the edge of a terrace. At night there is nothing but the sound of the river and bright stars overhead; at dawn we wake to the chorus of native birds. When the weather is fine (admittedly a big assumption), it is the most beautiful place in a beautiful country. I spent a quiet Christmas reading, painting, doing a little forestry work, hearing a few grumbles from local farmers and generally recharging the batteries. The markets were quiet, and we ended 2007 anxious but hoping that the worst was now behind us.

The new year began with the traditional Reserve Bank governor's speech to the Employers' Chamber of Commerce in the southern city of Christchurch. At that time of year the city is warm and, flying in, you are treated to a stupendous view of the Southern Alps. I was in good spirits as I greeted an enthusiastic audience and a strong contingent of reporters. My topic this year was how New Zealand was coping with huge price shocks. Given the size of the oil, commodity, asset, exchange rate and other price rises we were experiencing, the answer was 'surprisingly well, but . . . .' There is always a 'but' in our speeches. This time it was not to do with the financial crisis: we were more worried about people thinking that this inflation would continue.

The next day, a Saturday, Jenny and I continued another tradition, attending the Wellington Anniversary Day horse race meeting at Trentham Racecourse. There, under a shady grove of oak trees, New Zealand Post pitches their marquee and plays host to the movers and shakers of New Zealand government and industry. I exchanged pleasantries with Prime Minister Helen Clark, several former prime ministers and Opposition Leader John Key. Everyone was talking about the crisis, and although few had inside knowledge, many held strong views. I was given a lot of free advice.

Inside knowledge increased our uncertainty. On the global scene there was more news: the Bank of America had just purchased a major ailing US bank, Countrywide Financial, for $4 billion. The Federal Reserve signalled its continuing concern by cutting interest rates further. We heard more gossip about financial instruments – not just subprime mortgages but a cluster of acronyms: ABSs, RMBSs, CDOs, CDSs.* Worries buzzed around the markets like flies. We saw this anxiety on our Reuters and Bloomberg screens and our traders and financial market people heard it on the phone and witnessed it in the trades. Everyone was trying to understand a new climate.

Then we started to see bottlenecks mounting in key markets. Monoline bond insurance, the extremely specialised market that insures bonds, was a key example. With mortgage prices dropping, the monoline industry could no longer handle all the risk it had been insuring. The credit rating agencies started to downgrade the monoline firms; in response, banks scrambled to reinsure or re-hedge their exposures. In early February, Federal Reserve Chairman Ben Bernanke publicly expressed his concern that bond insurers could have an adverse effect on financial markets and the economy. The contagion was spreading.

On 13 March, Bear Stearns, Wall Street's fifth largest investment bank, hit the headlines with a massive $15 billion devaluation of assets. Rumours about their financial problems had seen their share price slashed.

The credit default swap (CDS) market provides a listing where anyone can see prices in real time, on screen, giving an estimate of the chance of a company defaulting. Bear Stearns had been heavily involved in subprime and other risky asset instruments and was losing value rapidly. Over the preceding weeks, Bear Stearns' CDS spreads (the price of insuring against default) had been steadily widening, and stockholders (including the company's own employees) started selling their shares. Bear Stearns' equity price plummeted, their market

---

* ABSs – asset-backed securities; RMBSs – residential mortgage-backed securities; CDOs – collateralised debt obligation; CDSs – credit default swaps.

capitalisation dropped and the chances of defaulting rose even higher – a self-fulfilling prophecy. The possibility of closure shocked the markets. Then the Federal Reserve, judging that this closure would cause so much turmoil in the inter-bank market that it would endanger other banks, surprised the markets further by stepping in and organising a rescue. They engineered a forced sale to JPMorgan Chase (in a deal backed by $30 billion of central bank loans), effectively closing the company in a controlled way.

For the first time American regulators had to confront the problem of what to do with a financial institution that is too big – or too complex, or too interconnected, or too politically important – to fail. It had long been recognised that the weaknesses of commercial banks could have domino effects, and banks were supervised to minimise these risks. But the investment banks, even the largest, had not been considered to pose a threat to the system itself. Bear Stearns forced the American Government to rethink its position.

Now other parts of the whole wobbly system of US mortgage lending started to show stress. Rumours were circulating about the two massive institutions, Fannie Mae and Freddie Mac, that between them own or guarantee a majority of American home mortgage borrowing. The government had wanted to use them as a crutch to prop up America's home borrowing in the downturn, but now they were looking very sick themselves. Their capital requirements were eased to allow them to lend more, but this was only a temporary solution. Within months the government had to assure the market that Fannie and Freddie would not be allowed to fail.

Every six months the financial markets department of the Reserve Bank assesses the state of New Zealand's financial system and writes up the results of its findings in a financial stability report. Once read only by the banks and a few geeky analysts, now the country's media eagerly awaited its publication.

From the seventh floor of the Reserve Bank, the team of half a dozen economists, financial analysts and regulators study the reports of financial health that they get, not just daily but sometimes by the minute, on the world's financial markets. We blend this with intelligence from our bank supervisors, our economic forecasters, our cash providers and the operators of New Zealand's wholesale payment-settlement system.

In early May 2008 we published our first *Financial Stability Report* of the year. Financial reporters crowded the Reserve Bank museum where we hold our press conferences. I described these events as the largest financial shocks since the Great Depression, but I also assured questioners that New Zealand's financial system was fundamentally sound – affected by the higher cost of world funding, but with little exposure to offshore risks, and holding appropriate capital buffers. Sitting alongside me, Grant Spencer announced the temporary assistance measures we were putting in place – a funding facility, and extended arrangements for securities – to reassure banks about the availability of credit.

Surprisingly, after a year of global financial crisis, the world economy was still running hot, with mounting imbalances and inflating prices. Strong growth, especially in China and the other big emerging economies (the BRICs – Brazil, Russia, India, China), was keeping commodity prices dangerously high. In the year to July 2008 the oil price had doubled, reaching the unheard-of level of US\$147 per barrel. This imposed big costs on us.

But financial matters were uppermost on our minds, our immediate problem was inflation: 4 per cent in the year to June, heading for 5 per cent in the year to September. I was keenly aware (and continually reminded by the Board) of my contractual responsibilities in the Policy Targets Agreement: to deliver inflation measured by the CPI in the 1–3 per cent range over the medium term. We forecast that inflation would soon reduce, but it had not yet. We therefore had a tough call to make when we met to review the official cash rate in July. Monetary policy cash rate cuts can take a long time to have an effect, and we were worried that the credit crunch would soon start to bite. But central banks such as that in Australia and the European Central Bank were still keeping rates high to counter inflationary pressures. By law, I make the official cash rate decision, but I have a formal OCR Advisory Group with half a dozen highly experienced Reserve Bankers and two outside members. Though not unanimous, there was a strong feeling in the Group that cutting the interest rate now would be an appropriate precautionary measure in case the financial situation worsened. I agreed and – to the surprise of some in the market – we began our cycle of OCR cuts. This was a clear demonstration of our belief that monetary policy be targeted at medium-term not short-term inflation pressures.

While working towards this decision in July, we had a long-planned celebration. In 1958, a little-known New Zealand economist called Bill Phillips had quietly published a paper on the relation between prices and economic activity (which became known as the 'Phillips curve'). It set the economic world alight and ultimately provided governments and central banks with a framework for thinking about price stability and economic stimulus. Led by Grant Scobie from the New Zealand Treasury, a number of us had been preparing an international conference to mark the paper's fifty-year anniversary. It was huge by our standards – the biggest economic conference ever held in the country. I was to give an after-dinner speech about Bill Phillips the man. He had been an extremely unusual person: an intellectual genius who had led the most engaging life. Born on a small farm in Depression-era New Zealand, he had taken a journey of discovery through the world, surviving horrific war imprisonment, inventing the first hydraulic model of the economy and developing a number of brilliant mathematical models as well as his most famous Phillips curve. As I prepared the story of his life, I wondered how Phillips, scarred by the Depression, might have viewed today's events.

A month later I was back in Jackson Hole for the annual meeting of the Federal Reserve. Ben Bernanke, choosing his words carefully, presented an increasingly bleak view of the US situation. He left straight after his talk and flew back to Washington to be close to the action. After he had gone, there was animated discussion. Jacob Frenkel, a well-known economist and formerly central bank governor in Israel, summed up, saying, 'We've spent the last ten years talking about imbalances building around the world. We all agreed those weren't sustainable. What did you expect?' Stan Fischer, Frenkel's successor at the Bank of Israel, pointed out that though this was the world's worst financial crisis since the 1930s, it was not yet the worst economic crisis. World growth had slowed, but this was by no means a recession. The economic picture was not sunny but, unlike the financial scene, it didn't look too dark.

That was the forecast I brought back from Jackson Hole at the end of August 2008. Two weeks later, after an eerie calm, the US investment banking storm broke.

CHAPTER 3

Bursts, Busts and Bailouts
September 2008

A crisis always looks clearer from the distance of time but, as August 2008 drew to a close, we sensed that something major was in the air. Earlier in the year we had seen a return to stability, and hoped the worst was over. The failure of Bear Stearns had shattered that prospect. Now, as we watched the markets, all the omens were bad – further failures looked inevitable. We had two questions: who would be hit next? And who would pay for the failures? In New York, London, Frankfurt, and across the world, bankers were making urgent phone calls, reassessing their balance sheets and looking at how to offset their risks. Regulators were calling in their front line supervisors, warning their treasuries, keeping in close touch with one another. From our distant vantage point in New Zealand, we watched events closely.

The market signals were becoming clearer by the day. For years, much of the trading in subprime and other toxic assets had been voluminous and transparently profitable. The risks to balance sheets and in special off-balance sheet investment entities set up to minimise capital requirements had been more obscure. As housing values fell, there were defaults on subprime mortgages and the prices of their derivative financial investments fell dramatically. This hit banks directly via their balance sheets and indirectly via weakened counterparties (the wide range of institutions that they had been doing business with).

Concealed as these 'tail' risks had been, at the start of September 2008 they began to show only too clearly on the markets' radar. On Wall Street, the stock prices of key listed financial firms began to fall. On other financial markets the CDS spreads were widening. Worst hit were the giant US investment banks that had been at the heart of the 'originate and distribute' model. Some years earlier a number of them had floated shares on the stock exchange, making many of their staff very rich. Now those employees were panicking and selling their shares. Worried that this indicated more bad news inside the firms, outside stockholders followed suit, and share prices tumbled. This in turn triggered special covenants (legal agreements setting conditions for lending), leading to more stress.

In the giant but curiously personalised world of Wall Street, what matters most to the titans of finance is the pecking order. After the failure of Bear Stearns, falling stock markets and ballooning CDS spreads pointed to the next in line: Lehman Brothers.

Fannie Mae and Freddie Mac, those unusual institutions set up by Franklin Delano Roosevelt in the Depression, needed a bailout. As guarantors of nearly half the American housing market (together they owned or guaranteed about $5.3 trillion worth of mortgages), they were in turn implicitly guaranteed by the US Government. The companies spent large amounts on lobbying in Washington to maintain close relationships with the Administration and Congress. Commentators had warned over the years that their arrangements with Washington would backfire on the taxpayer. In July, a rescue package from the Fed and Congress had given the government authority to offer the two companies unlimited liquidity and to buy their shares. Despite this backing, the values of their mortgage portfolios continued to fall.

On 7 September the government placed the two companies into federal conservatorship (a legal arrangement allowing for temporary government control), pledging up to $200 billion in capital. Announcing one of the largest bailouts in American history, US Treasury Secretary Henry Paulson justified the decision on the basis of 'systemic risk', declaring, 'Fannie Mae and Freddie Mac are so large and so interwoven in our financial system that a failure of either of them would cause great turmoil in our financial markets here at home and around the globe.' Bernanke and Paulson were criticised for their intervention by both Democrats and Republicans, those on the right disliking the interference in the market and the disregard of moral hazard (the principle that people should pay for the consequences of their risky actions), those on the left unhappy with the use of taxpayers' money.

Most of the major investment banks were now in trouble, with their yields spreading on the credit-default swap market and their share prices plummeting. On Wednesday, 10 September, Wall Street investment bank Lehman Brothers, the largest underwriter of subprime mortgage-backed securities, announced a $3.9 billion loss in the third quarter. A run on its liabilities seemed to be under way, its liquidity was vanishing and its stock price tumbling. On Thursday, 11 September, Tim Geithner, then president of the New York Federal Reserve, the arm of the US Fed that oversees financial markets, warned Ben Bernanke and Hank Paulson that the company looked unlikely to open for business the following Monday.

We in New Zealand had dealt with stock market crashes before. This time, we had had earlier warnings. Since the beginning of the subprime crisis the previous year, at the Reserve Bank we had reviewed our own risks and considered the likely implications for the country. There is nothing like a hint of fear in the air to invigorate bank regulators: we had smartened up our monitoring processes and were keeping closer to the banks. We felt that we understood their risks: they looked reasonably well managed and New Zealand did not have major investment bank operations.

The Bank had been recruiting to bolster our bank monitoring teams, and I was pleased with the quality of the people we had attracted. When banks are booming, they offer very high salaries and bonuses to qualified people with a good knowledge of balance sheets and risks. A public agency like the Reserve Bank, which pays public sector salaries and no bonuses, can find it hard to compete. But in contrast to some of the bureaucratic regulatory giants overseas, we have a reputation for being a good employer. In our tiny but world-leading central bank, staff can gain useful experience and their views are valued and heard. Their work is directly helping New Zealand, so staff are very motivated. We had recently appointed a new regulator, Toby Fiennes, to head our prudential supervision team. Toby brought with him wide experience at the Bank of England and the Financial Services Authority.

Many overseas bank regulators spend their time sitting inside their target banks, poring over customer accounts. We have a more light-handed touch. We rely on a deep understanding of bank processes and we require a considerable amount of information which must be signed off by their directors. So far this system has worked well.

In a crisis the other key part of the Bank is our financial markets department. Here the traders sit all day (and sometimes evenings) in front of computer screens, monitoring and transacting in the financial markets. In the big banks you find large rooms with row after row of desks and traders, enlivened by a few attempts at personalisation: flags, football banners, photos and a deal tombstone or two commemorating a significant trade. Big television screens – for some reason often showing American basketball games – dominate the room. There is a feeling of testosterone in the air and a steady hum of voices, an occasional shout of triumph or moan of despair, as deals come and go.

The trading space at the Reserve Bank of New Zealand is low key in comparison. The screens are there, and so too are the banners and family photos. But traders in a central bank behave differently – to manage our balance sheet they need to be calmer, more reflective and always aware of risk. For its size, the Reserve Bank has a very large balance sheet (assets and liabilities) – its assets currently totalling about $25 billion. Part of this is to back New Zealand's currency issuance, part to back up the overnight liquidity requirements of the domestic market and part to manage our foreign currency.

Our FX traders are managed by Simon Tyler, universally known as 'Moose' for reasons no one can now recall. Quiet, but highly respected inside and outside the bank, he has spent a career in trading banks and is unusual among traders in being an instinctive leader. His leadership skills and top market contacts are crucial in a crisis. Simon oversees a small team of traders, another team who regulate the liquidity of our overnight banking market and a third group, the most technical of them all, who work out the risk exposures on the balance sheet and how to ensure they do not go beyond set limits. The three teams would be tested severely in weeks to come.

Together with Grant Spencer, Don Abel and John McDermott, the other governors of the Reserve Bank, Simon Tyler and Toby Fiennes made up the key team over the coming months as we looked at what was happening offshore, struggled to understand what we learned and pondered how to insulate our financial system from the worst disruptions. The first week of September was a time of hurried meetings and stock-takes. Complicating the landscape, I had to make another decision on the official cash rate, though that would not be announced till the following week.

If only, when crisis strikes, one were able to clear one's diary and mind to focus on nothing else. Life is not like that. I had been suffering from a niggling toothache for some time and during that fateful first week of September I had to find time for a root canal operation. My orthodontist was super-modern and competent. After the first jaw-jabbing injections had taken effect, I lay back in the dentist's chair for a whole hour and a half with nothing to disturb me but the ceiling. As the drills, suction hoses and other dental instruments passed in and out of my mouth, I tried to make sense of events: first subprime, then Northern Rock, then Bear Stearns, then Lehman, then ... what?

I had been keeping in close contact with the secretary to the New Zealand Treasury, John Whitehead. I knew John well from the years we had worked together at Treasury. Soft-spoken, well-mannered, considerate and thoughtful, John marshalled economic advice for the Minister of Finance and kept an eye on public service spending. Apart from issuing and managing public debt, the Treasury did not play a direct role in the New Zealand financial markets. However, we knew that if government financial support were ever needed by the markets, Treasury would have to be in the middle of the decision-making. While in some countries the relationship between the central bank and the treasury is difficult, even hostile, both John and I knew that in a small vulnerable country institutions had to work together. In good years we had built an atmosphere of trust and cooperation that was to stand us well in bad years.

The recipient of Treasury's economic advice, the Minister of Finance, is to be found when in Wellington in the Beehive, that circular wedding cake of a building, reputedly first designed by Sir Basil Spence on a paper napkin in a Wellington restaurant in the 1970s. Tightened security after the events of 9/11 now means that officials negotiate a phalanx of security guards and X-ray machines to enter the building, filing past visiting tourists, lobbyists and parties of school children. The office of the Minister of Finance is on the seventh floor. Like other ministerial offices it is tasteful but not grand, with bookcases, a New Zealand flag, a desk and a larger table for official meetings.

Finance Minister since 1999, Dr Cullen brought to his role considerable experience, hugely important in a time of crisis. He had dealt with the Air New Zealand failures, the impact of the 9/11 bombings and the financial rescue of New Zealand Rail. Cerebral, intensely political, Michael Cullen liked nothing so much as a verbal stoush in Parliament – something at which he excelled. Even during a crisis his fast wit and character assassination could have us in stitches. At other times he would become silent, retreat into his office and listen to classical music behind the closed door. Though he valued senior officials like John and myself, he never accepted any advice without critically contesting it.

On 3 September Michael Cullen, John Whitehead and I had dinner at the Reserve Bank. We had found that an occasional meal together was a good chance to talk things over without the usual tight agenda, queue of officials outside the door and private secretary taking minutes. These dinners were simple enough affairs – salad, a meat dish and a good New Zealand red wine. In our positions, fancy food is to be minimised or avoided altogether – we have to keep an eye on our lifestyles, our waistlines and our watches. On the specifics of our conversations that evening, I will not break confidence. It is enough to say that we could see the direction Wall Street was heading and we were worried about the consequences for New Zealand.

Dr Cullen had another problem, a political one. In a couple of months New Zealand would be heading to the polls in a general election. New Zealand senior official appointees such as John and I are completely neutral in politics – we serve with the same professionalism and enthusiasm whomever the public elects. I myself have worked for four Ministers of Finance and many other associate Ministers from a number of political parties. Though we would not generally discuss politics in such meetings, now we had to acknowledge that the risks of political instability over the next few months could make a crisis harder to manage.

As the first week of September passed and events accelerated behind closed doors in New York and Washington, we in Wellington were more focused on the slowing New Zealand economy. Every day at 8.30 a.m., our financial markets team holds a briefing on overnight developments in the world's markets. These briefings were now crucial. I also regularly talked things over with Dr Arthur Grimes, a top economist who used to work at the Reserve Bank and now chairs the Reserve Bank Board. Normally we do not consult on short-term financial matters, but now I needed his counsel.

That week we were due to release our monetary policy decision on 11 September. It was very difficult to know just how the Lehman problem was going to hurt the US economy, and how that would affect us. Quite apart from Lehman, our economic forecasts had significantly weakened over the past three months. We now expected a much flatter growth path; there was even a possibility that growth could drop to zero. As a consequence, the OCR Advisory Group recommended that I cut rates by a larger than usual 50 points to 7.5 per cent. Given the weakness of the economic forecast and the fallout from Lehman, I could only agree.

It has long been our custom to brief Ministers on our macro-economic forecasts before the announcement date, but not to tell them of our OCR decision until the morning of the announcement. Two days before the OCR was released, I went with John McDermott, our chief economist, to see the Prime Minister in her ninth-floor office suite with its view over the harbour. No one was looking at the view today.

I have known Helen Clark for a long time. In my first year at the University of Auckland, a time when I thought I was studying to be a historian, she was the girl who sat in the front row of the political studies lecture theatre, rapt in the lectures. We were not close, but we had always had a good professional relationship.

With her in her office were her chief of staff, Heather Simpson, and her department head, Maarten Wevers. There was a certain tension in the air as we discussed what might lie ahead.

Released on 12 September, our big OCR cut took the markets and the media by surprise. They generally approved: 'Bollard swings the big axe', said the *Dominion Post*; and 'Chop, chop, Bollard doubles the cut: Global market turmoil behind double cut', cried the *New Zealand Herald*. *Monetary Policy Statement* day is always very busy for the Reserve Bank, so I was not happy when, after an interrupted night, I woke to a migraine headache, obviously brought on by stress. I struggled through the press conference that morning, walked to the Television New Zealand studio to record an interview and gave several more phone interviews with Bloomberg TV and CNBC. With no time for lunch, I visited my doctor for some extra strong painkillers. Then it was off to Parliament to appear before the Finance and Expenditure Committee as they examined the *Monetary Policy Statement*. I tried to sound calm, authoritative and positive, even as Wall Street slept and the migraine pain rattled around in my head. Following a grilling from Mary Wilson for Radio New Zealand, I finally felt I could face no more. Sandy Anderson, my assistant, cancelled my afternoon trip to Auckland, where I was due to talk to business audiences, and Grant Spencer stepped in.

I crawled home, shut the curtains in the bedroom, swallowed more painkillers, pulled a pillow over my face and tried to sleep. There I stayed through Friday and Saturday, waiting for the infernal throbbing behind my ears to abate and gloomily contemplating what might lie ahead – but not imagining what was then unfolding on Wall Street.

The global markets and financial system were now far more fragile than they had been in March when Bear Stearns faltered. Realising Lehman's collapse could be catastrophic, Bernanke, Paulson and Geithner urgently set about trying to find a buyer before the markets opened on Monday. Paulson, frustrated by Lehman's failure to secure a buyer or major investor over the summer, had himself approached two serious contenders, the Bank of America and a British bank, Barclays. Feeling the heat over the bailout of Fannie Mae and Freddie Mac the previous week, he publicly ruled out any government funding.

The events of the weekend that led to Lehman's collapse were unknown to the world at the time, but over the following year I read and heard various accounts of what happened behind the scene. Of these, none is as revealing as James B. Stewart's article 'Eight Days: The Battle to Save the American Financial System' in *The New Yorker*, recounting the backroom efforts and dramatic developments from the points of view of key players.

Stewart describes how, over breakfast on Friday, 12 September, Bernanke and Paulson discussed a 'private sector' solution, whereby the buyer would receive financing for Lehman's troubled assets not from the government but from a consortium of banks. These banks were expected to put their differences aside and act together for the common good, knowing that the failure of Lehman would jeopardise them all. At a meeting at the New York Federal Reserve that evening, Geithner put the proposal to Wall Street CEOs and representatives of several European banks. Paulson told them there would be no public money. He later told Stewart, 'We said this publicly. We repeated it when these guys came in. But to ourselves we said, "If there's a chance to put in public money and avert a disaster, we're open to it."' He reminded the bankers that Lehman was unlikely to open for business on Monday morning – they had just 48 hours to resolve the issue.

The next day was Saturday, 13 September. When the Wall Street CEOs reassembled to work out a 'private solution' for the toxic assets, Barclays seemed the most likely buyer while the Bank of America was still a possibility. But later that day, a valuation team led by Goldman Sachs and Credit Suisse informed the CEOs that the 'hole' in Lehman's balance sheet appeared to amount to tens of billions of dollars. As one participant told Stewart, 'The air kind of went out of the room.'

Investment bank Merrill Lynch, which had written down $40 billion of assets in the past year because of bad mortgage debt, looked to be next in line. Its CEO, John Thain, presented Ken Lewis, CEO of Bank of America, with a share proposal. Lewis turned it down: he wanted to buy Merrill Lynch outright.

Meanwhile, earlier on Saturday an even more serious crisis emerged. American International Group (AIG), America's biggest insurance company, was facing a massive liquidity crisis and was to be downgraded by all three major rating agencies on Monday. A pioneer in credit-default swaps and one of their largest issuers, AIG had hundreds of billions of dollars in exposure. The risk from its swap portfolio had been thought minimal and the company hadn't hedged enough. However, through the northern summer of 2008, as increasing numbers of borrowers couldn't pay their loans, default rates rose, and the rating agencies began a wholesale downgrade of mortgage-backed securities. AIG then had to provide larger amounts of collateral to buyers of its swaps. How would the insurance company come up with the cash?

Unaware of this crisis until then, Paulson summoned AIG's chief executive Robert Willumstad to the New York Fed that afternoon. Willumstad confirmed the company's liquidity crisis but was optimistic it could meet the cash demand in the short term by freeing up some of its enormous assets. But later that evening, the likelihood of a Lehman bankruptcy drastically affected AIG's outlook. According to Stewart, Willumstad estimated that AIG now needed $40 billion, twice the figure he mentioned earlier in the day. He would need government support to raise such a sum. He was told then that there would be none. Back at Lehman, without a government guarantee to cover the value of the bank's mortgaged-backed assets, negotiations with Barclays Bank broke down. The only way left to save Lehman was for the government to nationalise the company but, according to Paulson, they did not have legal authority to do that – and with a bank run already under way, it was not practical.

The bank was left to collapse. On the Sunday afternoon police cordoned off the Lehman Brothers building and employees left with cartons of belongings. Shortly before one o'clock in the early hours of Monday, 15 September, Lehman filed for bankruptcy.

The same day, Bank of America bought Merrill Lynch for $50 billion. After Bear Stearns and Lehman, it was the third of the five top United States investment banks to fall victim to the credit crunch. Wall Street investment banks Morgan Stanley and Goldman Sachs, now the only big independent investment banks on Wall Street, saw their shares plummet as panic continued among investors.

In New Zealand on the afternoon of 15 September we heard the shocking triple announcements that Merrill Lynch had been sold, AIG had been downgraded and – most stunning of all – that Lehman had filed for bankruptcy. Hank Paulson had insisted that these events take place before the world markets opened for business, by which he meant Asian stock markets. But he had forgotten that New Zealand opens some hours earlier – the first in the world – and the stock market in our region took a battering. Lehman was the first major bank to collapse because of the financial crisis, and the biggest Chapter 11 bankruptcy ever. (The last major Chapter 11 filing in the United States had been Enron, but Lehman had a far bigger balance sheet.)

Shock waves were felt around the world as the Lehman collapse led to other financial institutions desperately trying to get out of Lehman's debt and paper. As panic spread, the payment and settlement systems that banks use to complete their transactions with each other were tested as never before, as huge amounts went through. Known as the 'plumbing', the payment and settlement system is crucial to a sound market, and we were about to see whether the new electronic structures would work as intended.

Unlike many central banks, the New Zealand Reserve Bank owns, operates and regulates the country's payment and settlement systems. Together the Austraclear New Zealand system and the Exchange Settlement Account System handle approximately $40 billion in transactions per day. We also belong to the Continuous Linked Settlement Bank (CLS), which handles most international foreign exchange transactions. The only central bank holding direct membership, New Zealand had been the first central bank in the world to join CLS. We had never seen it under major stress. The day after Lehman's collapse, CLS handled its greatest ever volume of transactions in a day and in New Zealand our local systems also handled a record amount. We worried about the effects of transactions jamming the system. Under these fragile conditions, slow or failed payments mean some banks are unable to on-pay other parties, with dangerous consequences for the whole banking system. Fortunately the system held up under the record flows.

On the other hand, the collapse of Lehman had led to a worldwide freeze in the markets for commercial paper, the short-term loans companies use to finance their operations. Twenty per cent or more of New Zealand bank funding comes from US and European commercial paper markets and now banks could not get renewals. That was a big worry for them – and for us.

The Reserve Bank provides the notes and coins that New Zealanders use every day, something that we normally take for granted. For emergencies, we hold extra stores of money in our vaults and offshore; a central bank cannot afford to run out of money. Unlike many central banks, we do not print our own notes; instead we buy supplies from printers overseas. The $100 note is New Zealand's highest denomination currency and what people use to withdraw large amounts. When Alan Boaden, our currency manager, reported that banks were ringing up and asking for urgent deliveries of $100 notes, it was an important signal and we responded swiftly. When we followed up the inquiries we heard disquieting stories from bank managers. Customers, hearing rumours about financial carnage overseas, were worried about the security of their money in our banks. They were going into branches and saying, 'We're not sure if our money's safe here, we want to take it out.' Some people were splitting their deposits between banks to lessen the risk. More disturbing were reports about depositors, often older people or recent immigrants, doing risky things like stuffing bundles of cash up the chimney or burying them in the garden.

We checked our stock of new $100 notes and reviewed our emergency holdings, kept in the vaults in our building below the pavement on The Terrace in Wellington. After some calculations, we decided they were sufficient for the present situation. A few years earlier, following the SARS and avian influenza scares, we had doubled our holdings of notes to be able to respond to a crisis-triggered run on cash. That decision now stood us in good stead. We were able to supply all the $100 notes that the banks wanted.

In emergency meetings throughout Monday, 15 September, and into the early hours of Tuesday morning, the New York Fed continued to try to find a solution to the impending failure of AIG. Potential buyers had backed off, syndicate efforts collapsed. At midnight Geithner asked the team that were working on a solution, 'Can we let it go?' In the small hours of the morning they reached consensus: the insurance giant was too deeply tied into the global financial system to be allowed to fail. On 17 September Geithner and Bernanke announced a US Government rescue loan of $85 billion, the biggest government intervention in the market since the 1930s. Bernanke justified it, explaining that the extent of the exposures of major banks around the world to AIG and the extreme fragility of the system meant that AIG's failure could have sparked a global banking panic. He added: 'If that had happened, it was not at all clear that we would have been able to stop the bleeding, given the resources and authorities we had at that time.' Scholar of the 1930s Depression, Bernanke well recognised the dangers. In an interview for *TIME* in December 2009 he reflected, 'We came very, very close to a depression. The markets were in anaphylactic shock.'

As rumours abounded in the markets, stocks and the US dollar tumbled, with banking shares, hardest hit. To try to reassure markets, the US Federal Reserve broadened its emergency lending scheme. On 16 September the Fed put $70 billion into credit markets, but with little evident effect. Now money market funds were also in trouble, including the venerable Reserve Management Company whose Primary Fund was exposed to Lehman's failure. Its value dropping below its liabilities, the Primary Fund 'broke the buck', causing a new money market run.

Recognising this 'pivotal moment for America's economy', on Friday, 19 September, President Bush addressed the public: 'Our system of free enterprise rests on the conviction that the federal government should interfere in the marketplace only when necessary. Given the precarious state of today's financial markets – and their vital importance to the daily lives of the American people – government intervention is not only warranted; it is essential.'

The Administration was preparing the Troubled Asset Relief Program (TARP) that would cost the taxpayer $700 billion. On 21 September, Goldman Sachs and Morgan Stanley, the last of the stand-alone investment banks on Wall Street, surrendered their independent status and became licensed bank holding companies.

It had been a horrendous fortnight, with the most significant change to the American financial system since the Depression. The relationship between government and big banks had altered, maybe forever. The surviving investment banks dived for cover, either merging with a major trading bank or applying directly for a government banking licence. The US Government had found itself in a position where it had to assume the credit risk from these banks, but had not yet worked out how to handle the risk, how to fund it and how to prevent the banks getting a free ride from the US taxpayer.

Now the financial markets changed their focus – they wanted to know how the US Government would finance this support for investment banks, and they turned their attention downstream to what are known as Main Street banks. Some of these banks, the ones that directly lend mortgages to American home-buyers and take deposits from American savers, were also in trouble. These banks do not have the international reach that Bear Stearns and Lehman had, but they are politically and economically embedded in heartland America. First to go was Washington Mutual Bank, a giant mortgage lender with assets valued at nearly a third of a trillion dollars. On 25 September it was closed by regulators, making it the largest US bank failure in history. It was then on-sold to JPMorgan Chase. A few days later another giant lender, Wachovia Bank, was on-sold to Citigroup, with US Government backing.

In the meantime, the TARP bill had been introduced to the US Congress, seeking approval for a massive amount of money to fund the financial rescues. The Treasury felt they had little option at this stage but to raise emergency funds, on an unprecedented scale, very quickly. However, in the dying days of the Bush Administration, with a presidential election due in November, the US Congress was in no mood to see such a huge hit on taxpayer written quickly into legislation. The media made the most of the conflict, playing up political differences and giving air time to the mavericks.

On Monday, 29 September, the unthinkable happened: the US House of Representatives rejected the rescue plan. Global markets went into convulsions. The US Standard & Poor's 500 Index (one of the main benchmarks for US stocks) closed down 8.8 per cent, its biggest one-day decline since the October 1987 stock market crash. We watched anxiously from New Zealand as stock prices plummeted further and companies wondered whether they could last the week. After desperate political manoeuvring behind the scenes, on Friday, 3 October, acting under urgency, the House finally passed the TARP, and temporary relief was in sight.

But this was too late to stop the plague that was already spreading through world markets. Europe was hit hard. In Britain and Ireland, further worry about the viability of banks prompted actions by both governments to try to prop up confidence in the system. Within a month the British Government had had to pump £37 billion capital into HBOS, the Royal Bank of Scotland and other banks, and was left controlling much of the country's banking system.

After a run on shares of HBOS, Britain's biggest mortgage lender, the UK Government induced Lloyds TSB to take it over in a £12 billion deal, creating a conglomerate holding nearly a third of the country's mortgages and savings. The Bank of England announced that it was putting funds totalling £28 billion into the financial system.

The European central banks injected a huge €35 billion into their banking system. In late September, the giant European banking and insurance company Fortis revealed that it too was in trouble. Helping it out was made harder by the fact that although Fortis was registered in

Belgium, its bigger operations were in the Netherlands and elsewhere. The Dutch and Belgian Governments argued publicly about what to do. A few days later the German Government had to commit €50 billion to save Hypo Bank, a big domestic lender.

And in Iceland, the tiny North Atlantic nation with three large and very entrepreneurial banks, the situation had imploded. Its government, faced with massive debts, started nationalising the banks, knowing that their liabilities were more than the government could afford. The markets showed no mercy. The Icelandic krona plummeted, and no one would do business in that currency at almost any price.

The days following the Lehman/Merrill Lynch/AIG news were deeply worrying. Like many central bankers, we struggled to understand what the crisis would mean for our own country. Would the fallout be limited to the big Northern Hemisphere investment banks or was this the start of a global financial meltdown? The growth of the internet means that thousands of bloggers now post their immediate reactions and analysis on a staggering array of websites. Hidden among them are valid information and expert views. We worked through these, trying to understand what had happened. I also consulted widely, talking to bank chiefs, John Whitehead and the head of the Prime Minister's Department, Maarten Wevers. I also talked to Glenn Stevens, knowledgeable and wise governor of the Reserve Bank of Australia. And when the Board of the Reserve Bank met in Wellington we abandoned our original agenda – to appraise my performance during the year and recommend my salary – and instead devoted most of the time to discussing the events offshore.

Still very unsure of how events would develop, I convened an evening crisis meeting of senior people on our staff. We would need all the skills of the experienced financial market traders, risk managers, bank regulators and economic forecasters in the months ahead.

It is always difficult for a central banker to know how to respond in a crisis. We have various tools that can be used to prop up a bank or to inject money into a system. Most important is the central banker's credibility, but this is a fragile asset – it must be used with great care. We thought now was the time. But what to say? We could say we thought the New Zealand banking system was robust, but saying this might only make people wonder. We could say that we would not allow any New Zealand financial institution to fail, but that might not be true. Instead, on Friday, 19 September, after the financial markets had opened, we issued an unusual press release: the Reserve Bank expressed its confidence in the New Zealand banking system, and said its staff were closely following developments in the United States and global financial markets. In addition the Reserve Bank stood ready to support any liquidity measures that might prove necessary for New Zealand's financial system. For all its generalities, the statement reassured the local markets – they accepted it at face value. It didn't sound like we were covering up weaknesses. None of the media asked what might trigger interventions. And we had another week or two to work out for ourselves just what our response might have to be.

Further bad news was still to hit us that month. We never know exactly where the economy is today. Our data is usually at least three months behind. On 26 September, Statistics New Zealand released the GDP figures for the June 2008 quarter: the economy had contracted by 0.2 per cent, caused initially by a drought in 2007. (The dry spell had been unusual – it hit dairy country instead of the East Coast sheep and cattle regions usually most susceptible to dry weather – and the resulting loss of dairy exports severely dented our GDP.) Following a negative number in the March quarter, we had had six months of negative growth: New Zealand was now officially in recession.

CHAPTER 4

A Very Bad Week in a Very Bad Month
October 2008

September was the cruellest month for Northern Hemisphere investment banks but, for us, October was to prove toughest.

On Tuesday, 7 October 2008, I arrived at work early and, as usual,
opened up the Reuters screen on my computer to see what Northern
Hemisphere carnage had occurred overnight. The international markets remained extremely volatile: hit heavily by losses from the US
investment banks, alarmed by the procrastination of the US Congress,
horrified as they watched the 'disease' spread across Europe.

My computer screen flickered to life, showing a weaker New Zealand
dollar and a further drop in the stock markets. This was unsurprising. But
I was shocked later in the day when the screen flashed the news that the
Australian Reserve Bank had cut cash rates by 100 basis points – both huge
and unprecedented. Two days later we heard that the US Federal Reserve,
the European Central Bank, the Bank of China, the Bank of England, the
Swiss and the Swedes were all cutting their interest rates by 50 points. This
big cut – incredibly difficult to synchronise – was probably the world's
largest central bank coordination ever. It would have been vital to ensure
that the markets did not get wind of the cut before the announcement.
There must have been intense, confidential late-night telephone calls,
probably using land lines for security reasons. (Did they ring us to ask if we
wanted to be part of it? No, I'm afraid that when the chips are down, New
Zealand is not big enough to count in these international interventions.)

The big central banks were hoping that this show of coordinated intent would provide banks with a stimulus and bring confidence back to the traders on Wall Street and in the City of London. However, the markets were not to be easily reassured. That day, glued to the electronic trading screens, we saw intense volatility in the foreign exchange markets, and prices in the equity markets continued to drop ominously. How far could this go?

In a crisis, bank regulators look forward to the weekend, because almost all the markets around the world close down, allowing time to take emergency actions behind closed doors. It was Friday, 10 October; we had scraped through to the end of a horrible week but, with various New Zealand developments brewing, there was to be no respite. I spent Saturday on the phone, thinking and planning. That evening, my wife and I attended Janáček's opera *Jenůfa*, a story of dysfunctional families in dysfunctional communities. I sat glumly through the long gloomy production, reassured by my BlackBerry turned to vibrate. As the inevitable tragic ending played out, I reflected on the mess we were in.

The Australian dollar was still falling sharply. The New Zealand dollar had had a better run – it was strong when measured against the Australian. Although volatile, as all currencies were, it was not getting what the markets refer to as 'trashed'. At the same time that the Australian dollar was taking a drubbing, it had been another shocking day on the Australian stock market. Australians hold more equities than we do and they watch the market values of their individual savings schemes very closely. The falling prices were reducing their wealth by the day and knocking their confidence. With a fairly new government in Canberra, the stock market was important not only financially but politically. We surmised that Premier Kevin Rudd would want to take action, but what? Would he consult us about it – and how might it affect New Zealand?

At the New Zealand Reserve Bank we had been on full alert all week. I had kept in close touch with Michael Cullen, who was very concerned and wanted to stay up to date on what was happening. We had been reporting that world financial markets were volatile and unpredictable but that, so far, things were holding up for us. We agreed that it was time to take the next step in case the crisis worsened. A small number of senior officials would work, very quietly, on preparing for a possible government intervention to guarantee bank deposits. It was crucial not to make this public; if word got out, it could have added to public anxiety and triggered exactly the bank run we were so anxious to prevent.

We felt compelled to be doubly prepared because of the signs of depositor nervousness we had seen two weeks earlier. So far the media hadn't picked up anything about a run on cash but any hint of such a story could have sparked rumours about unsafe banks and become the catalyst for a bank panic. When panic starts it is very hard to stop. Television images of crowds gathering outside the British offices of the failing bank, Northern Rock, only a year earlier, still haunted us. So far in New Zealand the value of withdrawn deposits was not huge – millions of dollars, to be sure, but only a small fraction of accounts on deposit. But we knew we had to be prepared for the worst.

With this in mind, we had set to work with our colleagues in Treasury to design a retail deposit guarantee scheme, whereby the government would guarantee people's deposits in banks, financial companies, building societies and credit unions up to some dollar cap. Initially this was to be kept extremely confidential so as not to alarm people. The rationale for this policy had its roots overseas. A week earlier, on the other side of the world, the troubles had come to a head in the Irish banking sector. As depositors in Ireland fretted about whether to pull their money out of the banks, the Irish Government announced a deposit guarantee scheme. But across the Irish Sea, British depositors grew increasingly worried about the safety of their deposits at home – would they move their money from British banks to guaranteed Irish banks? Fearing this, the UK Government responded quickly with a guarantee scheme of their own. In a domino effect, this caused Australian banks to worry that they would in turn lose funds to the British scheme. It is impossible for a small country like New Zealand to escape such chain reactions – a similar pattern of behaviour had helped drive the world into the Depression of the 1930s. Despite all the distortions inherent in guarantee schemes, it was time for us to consider one in New Zealand.

Obstacles lay ahead. The Labour-led Government, aware it was facing an uphill battle to win a fourth term, had set a general election date for 8 November. Everything, including the global crisis, took on a domestic political hue. In light of the Northern Hemisphere events, the government wanted to announce on Sunday, 12 October, as part of the launch of the Labour Party's election campaign, that it would consider a deposit guarantee scheme. We suggested to the Minister that making the policy public at another time would be less pointed politically, but his view was that to delay was risky.

We also worried intensely about the design of the scheme itself: it could cost the taxpayer heavily. Normally such a scheme would be debated in Parliament as part of the proper scrutiny of public funds. But Parliament had been dissolved for the election. We advised the Minister that we felt it would be proper to brief the main Opposition Members of Parliament, the National Party's John Key and Bill English. Dr Cullen agreed to our doing that, but only after the announcement had taken place.

We spent a day or two working out some careful wording that the Prime Minister could write into her speech for the Sunday afternoon. Acting Treasury Secretary Peter Bushnell and I were operating together as a team on the scheme. (The Reserve Bank would not have direct powers over the scheme, but would have to advise Treasury and the Minister of Finance over much to do with it.) His boss, John Whitehead, and my own deputy, Grant Spencer, were attending IMF meetings in Washington, which meant many long-distance phone calls. Our colleagues' news from Washington was not reassuring. In a fog of rumour, other countries seemed to be considering bank guarantees, rescues and insurances.

In the meantime, Prime Minister Helen Clark was mapping out precisely what she could say. She had learnt from other economic crises, such as the Air New Zealand rescue, to cast her messages carefully. There is a fine line between reassuring the public in a way which risks misleading them on one hand and scaring them on the other. I had a couple of conversations with her on the phone and she had texted parts of her speech to me on Friday night and again on Saturday as she worked the message into her speech. It had to be worded just so.

On Sunday morning, I heard an informed rumour that the Australian Government was considering announcing an immediate guarantee for their banks. Was this just one of the many stories that were floating about? I could not get confirmation. Then, a short time before the Prime Minister was to give her speech, she had a phone call from Kevin Rudd. He was planning a comprehensive guarantee for their banks and, moreover, he was announcing it that afternoon. What was she going to do?

This presented us with an immediate problem. Helen Clark was about to speak in front of a roomful of journalists and television cameras. She had planned to say only that we were *considering* a guarantee scheme. Because it was a party political occasion, it was not appropriate for any government officials to be present, and she could not get policy advice. We quickly arranged another phone call: the Prime Minister would announce a concrete guarantee scheme, active immediately. Inevitably that announcement overwhelmed the rest of the Labour Party's election launch. Michael Cullen was to give more details later that day.

Dr Cullen arranged a telephone conference with me, Heather Simpson and a few other officials to discuss the specifics of our scheme. The details of the Australian version were still unclear, but it sounded like it might be very generous. This could potentially cost the Australian Government a lot, but they were interested in sheltering shareholders in the banks as well as consumers. On our side, we decided to cap the guarantee and calculated a risk-based price for access to it. If a financial institution wanted to be included, they would have to pay for coverage based on how risky their balance sheet looked, as measured by credit rating agencies. We knew we would face all sorts of distortions as the scheme proceeded, but this seemed an equitable and efficient way to start.

In the meantime, we kept piecing together the likely parameters of the Australian scheme. The more Minister Cullen heard, the more concerned he became. He now wanted to introduce a more generous guarantee, as the Australian one apparently would be. Moreover, he was worried that New Zealand building societies and credit unions would be unable to afford a risk-based fee, and consequently he thought the scheme should have free entry. This changed the economics considerably: such a plan would be very costly and would leave the way open for entrepreneurial finance companies to undertake risky investments at taxpayers' expense. At my urging, Dr Cullen agreed to hold yet another conference call. The arguments were many. Suffice to say that, in the end, the Minister decided we would charge fees only on the amount of institutions' deposits above $5 billion. That would affect only the four big banks and Kiwibank. We knew this would cause distortions, but there was no perfect solution.

Though neither I nor my colleagues were very happy about New Zealand taxpayers having to guarantee bank deposits – it's not what we worked for – we had to enact the policy. Following an emergency meeting of senior Reserve Bank and Treasury people in our building on early Sunday morning, at the Treasury building a combined group of staff members worked on the guarantee scheme through the day. I had gone home, preferring to talk to the politicians from the quiet of my study, but returned that afternoon after the Prime Minister's announcements to check how things were progressing. Getting into the Treasury building on the weekend can be tricky, but when I arrived on the ninth floor I found a cluster of jeans-clad Reserve Bank and Treasury people, called in from their normal weekend activities, milling around in a hastily organised war room with stacks of paper, laptops and old pizza packets and coffee cups cluttering the central table. They all knew the situation was urgent but none of them had ever had to work through a crisis like this before.

I took on the job of coordinating their roles using a whiteboard: Who is doing what? What are the key parts of the design? Who is working out prices? What do we know about all the affected institutions? What about the website? How do we handle inquiries? And so on. After a few hours, fuelled by more coffee and pizza, the chaos gradually lessened and the whiteboard design started to come together. Now we needed heavyweight legal advice. We had a number of lawyers in the room – ours from the Reserve Bank, several from Treasury and another key specialist who had rushed back from a weekend in Taihape. They had to draft the contracts for the banks and finance companies to sign. We needed to be meticulous: we were acutely aware that the taxpayer could end up paying out very large sums to failed institutions.

Though we had only back-of-the envelope calculations, a hypothetical worst-case event looked likely to cost billions, not millions, of dollars. And at the same time we had to be extremely cautious about our use of the emergency powers (to disburse public moneys) that the Minister of Finance held under the Public Finance Act. We could not afford a constitutional crisis as well as a financial one.

The moment Helen Clark had announced the guarantee, the wires lit up with media and banks wanting immediate clarification. As soon as details had been agreed, we posted them on our website. (I was proud that we managed to do this so speedily; it took the Australians a few weeks to post comparable information.) Late Sunday night, I called Don Abel, assistant governor and head of operations, and he activated our emergency 0800 number. By seven o'clock the next morning it was ready to operate. We had two phone lines, one for people who were worried – like pensioners wanting to know if their money was safe – and the other for institutions who wanted to know if they would be covered. Calls from the latter group were taken by in-house specialists who worked around the clock. To field calls from the first group, we emailed staff in the Reserve Bank asking, 'Who wants to be a call centre operator for a day?' We had volunteers from all departments, gave them a quick training, provided a question and answer guide and got them started. Many of them enjoyed being part of the emergency response. And the lines were buzzing. That first Monday we fielded about 1000 calls. There was also huge media interest, including considerable international attention, inquiries from the news agencies on Wall Street and from the credit agencies. That worried me. We would have preferred to present a picture of business as usual. Some hope!

We had vigorous protests and table-thumping from the four Australian banks in New Zealand, indignant about being singled out to pay fees. But having dealt with them for six years as bank regulator, I have become hardened to some of their arguments. I also received a couple of angry phone calls from heads of the parent banks in Australia accusing us of anti-Australian prejudice. They would say things like that to me that they would not say directly to the Minister. I listened to their angry remarks, gave them a chance to pass on their views and let them vent their feelings, but I had to remind myself to be professional and stay cool. Our message to them was straightforward: 'We do light-handed regulation in New Zealand and we've never said the government stands behind the banks. You've just been given the possibility of a government guarantee. If you don't want it, that's up to you, but if you do, you had better sign up.' Their response was, 'But it's not fair, because you are charging only the big banks', and this was largely true. The issue behind this was bank funding. The big four have historically run their businesses based on short-term foreign loans from overseas, now a very vulnerable way of operating. They were feeling pain. In addition, we wanted the New Zealand branches to involve their parent banks and get funding support from them. The banks did not much like this message, but they understood it. The unspoken subtext of our message to the banks was that they had enjoyed many years of good returns in New Zealand, but now had to prepare for times to be tougher.

Other distortions in the scheme also provoked angry responses. We had had to include the non-banks; otherwise by Monday morning every finance company, building society and credit union in the country could have seen depositors withdrawing funds and putting them into guaranteed banks. Now that some financial institutions had a free guarantee, it angered the banks who saw it as unfair. And allowing finance companies to have a free ride meant other potential problems. From 2006 we had seen a clean-out of finance companies, beginning with the weakest property development companies going bust. We had to find legal ways of making sure none of these failures worked its way into the guarantee scheme, thus recovering profitability at the taxpayers' expense. A number of meetings followed. A week or so later we had further discussions with the Minister. My memory is of joining a conference call on my cellphone from a rental car in a carpark at Auckland Airport. Dr Cullen agreed to charge finance companies and savings institutions for guaranteeing any new business they took on. That helped limit the distortions, and Treasury started the onerous process of revising all the deeds.

We were also aware there would be boundary problems around the scheme. One such problem concerned people who did not have deposits but had put funds into collective investment schemes, invested in 'cash-like' assets. Initially it looked like they would not be covered by the government guarantee, and this risked withdrawals. We went back and made technical adjustments to clarify this class of investor, although some of these decisions later had to be revisited due to legal complexities. Finally, we had to deal with irate businesses writing, phoning and emailing, saying, 'We won't be able to raise commercial paper on the domestic market because we're not guaranteed, and will be at a disadvantage.' Even experienced business people get emotional at such worrying times. In the event, the local commercial paper market didn't turn out to be much of a problem.

After our intense weekend, by Monday, 13 October, we were exhausted, but there was no let-up. That morning, Peter Bushnell and I had to update the Leader of the Opposition. In constitutional terms, things were delicate: a global financial crisis, banks failing overseas, worried people taking cash out of banks in New Zealand, an emergency government guarantee that might use billions of dollars of public funds, no chance for Parliament to debate it and an election campaign in process, with the polls pointing to a likely change in government.

Peter and I climbed the marble and cast-iron staircase in Parliament Buildings to the restored Opposition Wing. As we neared the door we were confronted by flashing camera lights and recorders – the parliamentary press gallery had figured out what was happening. Pushing our way through the jostle of journalists, we reached John Key's office.

Sitting side by side on a pale yellow sofa, the Leader of the Opposition and the shadow Minister of Finance, Bill English, listened intently to our briefing. It was tricky ground for us – as public servants we had to balance the confidentiality of the government with the conventions of public information and, above all, not get politically engaged. The meeting went well – the two National Party politicians listened with interest, questioned us on some points and thanked us for the information. This was to be the model for future briefings in the fraught weeks ahead. Neither the Government nor the Opposition sought to make political capital out of a very fragile situation.

Throughout the crisis I had been keeping in touch with Dr Arthur Grimes, chairman of the Reserve Bank Board. The Board meets outside Wellington from time to time. Our next Board meeting was to be held that Thursday in Timaru. We considered moving it back to Wellington in case I got called away, but eventually decided to go ahead as planned.

I flew in to Timaru early and arrived at the motel where we were to hold the meeting. Needing some time by myself, I walked into town, found a pleasant café on High Street and pulled out the little sketch book that I carry with me. While I painted a little watercolour of the 1950s shop façades, I pondered on how to present the story of the turbulent week to the Board.

Around the board table, the directors were not happy. They had read about the guarantee scheme and they considered it risky, mispriced and distorting. I had to agree but argued that, more importantly, it had stopped an incipient bank run. Normally in the month of October we issue around 150,000 $100 notes. In October 2008 we issued about seven times that amount.

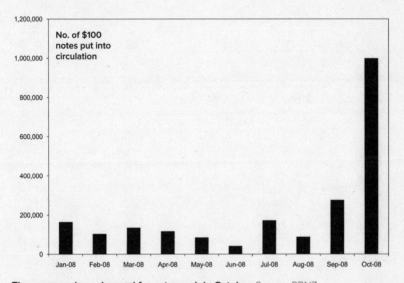

No. of $100 notes put into circulation

There was a sharp demand for extra cash in October. Source: RBNZ

I had to leave the meeting early to get a plane back, and as we headed to Wellington airport through the turbulent spring air, I wondered if we could have done anything better.

The next day we held an internal staff briefing. Every month, a hundred or so Reserve Bank staff gather on the second floor to hear what is happening elsewhere in the Bank. We use these meetings as a way to unify the staff from different departments and to motivate them. This time there was only one topic: the crisis. The room was packed. I handed the microphone to staff who had been running the call centre. One talked about being on the phone late at night listening to people yelling and crying at the other end.

Some of our own staff were now under stress. They had been working long hours, running on adrenalin – that can be dangerous. Listening to the stories, I wondered just how long this could go on.

CHAPTER 5

The Contagion Spreads
October–December 2008

We had now lived through the biggest shock to the financial system since the Great Depression. But a financial shock of this magnitude was clearly also going to cause significant economic damage. This effect first showed in the large, northern, developed economies with the biggest financial sectors. The festering finance problems were flowing into the non-financial sectors, what we call the 'real economy'. This cause and effect could be seen most clearly in the world's stock markets.

By the end of October 2008, the equity markets around the world had lost approximately half of their value from the beginning of the year. This loss – about $30 trillion US – was the biggest the world had ever seen. During the 1929 Depression, stock prices had dropped deeper, over a longer period, but publicly listed companies had then been a much smaller part of the economy and did not figure in most people's savings. Now, with equity prices plummeting and the bad news leaching into the real economy, it was no longer just traders and investment bankers who were worried about their jobs and bonuses. We started to see profit downgrades in big companies. From Detroit, we heard about the woes of the American auto industry. On the other side of the United States, Silicon Valley giants were losing sales and profits. Fears of the financial crisis spreading to the wider US economy were confirmed when on 15 October the Dow Jones index dropped 8 per cent on retail shares – its biggest fall since 26 October 1987.

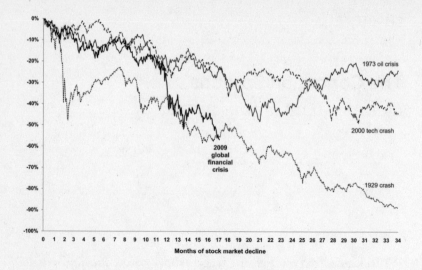

0% -10% -20% -30% -40% -50% -60% -70% -80% -90% -100%

1973 oil crisis

2000 tech crash

2009 global financial crisis

1929 crash

0 1 2 3 4 5 6 7 8 9 10 11 12 13 14 15 16 17 18 19 20 21 22 23 24 25 26 27 28 29 30 31 32 33 34

Months of stock market decline

This time the American stock market decline looked bad: in February 2009 we were confronted with a very gloomy picture. As it turned out, the Standard & Poor's 500 Index was reaching its trough at that point and, rather than following the gloomy track of the 1930s, was about to recover. Source: www.dshort.com

At the end of October the Fed cut interest rates by 50 basis points to 1 per cent as new data showed the US economy was shrinking further. Alarmed governments were also springing into action. The UK's Financial Services Authority raised the limit of guaranteed deposits to £50,000; governments in Germany, the UK, France, Italy and Ireland guaranteed bank accounts; Germany announced a €50 billion plan to save one of the country's biggest banks (Hypo Real Estate); and the Icelandic Government took control of its three major banks whose collapse, relative to the size of the economy, was by some accounts the largest suffered by any country in economic history.

On a trip to Washington earlier in the year, I had visited the US Treasury. On Pennsylvania Avenue, close to the White House, the marble and granite Treasury Building with its monolithic columns is a national icon. There I talked to a number of senior officials and walked down long corridors decorated with stern black-and-white photographs of successive

Treasury secretaries, among them Henry Morgenthau, who led in the 1930s Franklin Roosevelt's desperate efforts to lever the United States out of Depression, and Harry Dexter White, an enigmatic and hostile man (later fingered as a Soviet spy) who battled John Maynard Keynes over the establishment of the International Monetary Fund, intended to ensure the world would never again come to financial disaster.

Of special historic interest is the ornate suite that had been President Andrew Johnson's executive office in the weeks after Abraham Lincoln's assassination. Here I met with several US under-secretaries, one of whom emphasised how worried he was about the whole financial house of cards. I asked him what more the US Government had planned to ease the situation. He said he hoped what they had done would be enough. I pushed him further. 'Gee,' he said, 'remember that come January twentieth, we are getting the shit out of here!'

For someone used to the Westminster system where senior officials are apolitical and hold their jobs through merit, this was a timely reminder: the United States was facing a major election. Officials were assuming there would be a new administration. And when the new government came into office, approximately four top layers of senior officials in Treasury would be replaced by new political appointees, irrespective of the experience and skills lost. Secretary Hank Paulson and his top officials would presumably go (though the senior Federal Reserve appointees would remain in place). Then the US Congress might take a year or more to approve replacements.

The US Election Campaign complicated matters hugely. It was a media circus with an old warrior, Senator John McCain, squaring off against a newcomer, Senator Barack Obama. We had seen politicians delay the TARP bill until members of Congress realised the crisis was too dangerous to turn to political advantage. Having been briefed by officials, both proposed reforms to financial regulation. They realised that they needed to respond to the crisis with great care. For once, the polls were united on the key issue for the American voter: the economy, the economy, the economy.

From Wellington we watched the US election unfold, gripped by its drama. The polls had pointed to a Democratic president and by 5 p.m.

our time on 5 November it was clear that the United States, by far the biggest economy in the world, hit hardest by the crisis, would have a new leader. The financial markets welcomed the clear election results. But there were mighty questions ahead: could this inexperienced new president meet the challenge? The markets soon decided the answer was 'conditionally, yes'. Would he appoint senior officials and advisers whom the market trusted? Keeping some Republicans and appointing the New York Federal Reserve president, Tim Geithner, to Treasury secretary, and ex-secretary and senior Harvard academic Larry Summers as director of the White House's National Economic Council, was met with guarded approval. How long would Congress take to approve them all? More than a year. And how could this huge democracy manage financial rescues and economic stimulus over the next two months, with a lame-duck, outgoing president still holding office? With difficulty – exasperating as this was for the rest of the world.

In the midst of the worldwide gloom, it was ironic to get a piece of news that reminded us how recently our economy had been overheating. On 21 October we received the official inflation statistics: the CPI recorded a 5.1 per cent rise for the year to September 2008, the highest rate for nearly two decades. On the face of it, this did not look good. New Zealand had been the first country in the world, twenty years previously, to introduce a formal inflation target; and I, the Reserve Bank Board and the markets took my target of 1–3 per cent in the medium term very seriously. Our forecasts saw inflation dropping in the year ahead but, as yet, we had not seen this borne out. What worried us most was a return to 1970s stagflation, destructive inflation without growth.

In our medium-term inflation-targeting regime we always look well ahead. However, it was something of an act of faith when, two days later, we decided to cut the OCR drastically. We could see the financial carnage on world markets, and though oil, commodities, housing and other asset prices were still strong, it seemed likely that economic disaster was on its way. We took a deep breath and on 23 October cut the OCR by 100 basis points, to 6.5 per cent, the biggest cut the Reserve

Bank had ever made. Cautious with our language, in our usual press release we cited 'the rapidly deteriorating outlook for world growth and heightening turbulence in financial markets' – carefully chosen words intended to alert but not panic the markets.

But I wanted to explain further the size of this cut, so we decided to call a press conference. This is unusual for OCR announcements and as such risked alarming the financial markets, causing further volatility. Fortunately, because other central banks had been taking similar radical actions, our move did not seem out of line. A large turn-out of from the press corps crammed into our briefing space. Even the hardest-bitten, cynical journalists today were serious and seemed to be looking for reassurance. I was asked why we had not cut rates a week earlier, following the other central banks. Our scheduled OCR was in fact well timed, as the markets' acceptance confirmed.

A few days later we were part of an international initiative. Previously the US Federal Reserve had put in place 'swap facilities', arrangements to exchange currencies in the event that the market seized up completely. Initially we were worried: Australian and other currencies had been included, but the New Zealand dollar was simply not important enough to be on the Fed's international radar.

New Zealand has always punched above its weight internationally, and we have long nurtured American contacts and friends. Many American economists have visited us, keen both to study the system which pioneered inflation targeting, fiscal responsibility legislation and other innovations, and to travel in a country made famous by its scenery and people. I recall sitting at an overseas conference alongside one of the world's top bankers who turned to me and said, 'When this crisis is over we are going to visit New Zealand. My favourite film ever is *Lord of the Rings*.' His wife leaned across: 'That fantasy stuff! My favourite film ever is *Whale Rider*.'

At a time like this we call on our friends for informal lobbying. It did the trick. By the end of the month we were able to announce that the New Zealand dollar had been added to the USD swap facilities, providing access to liquidity worth up to US$15 billion. Shortly after this, Ben Bernanke was testifying to the US Congress when New

Zealand's inclusion in the facility was attacked by US Congressman Alan Grayson, who wanted to know what the US Government was doing lending taxpayers' money to a tiny inconsequential country at the other end of the world. Bernanke tried to explain that this was not a loan paid for by the United States; rather, it was a facility intended to broaden the market by enabling dollars to move between the two currencies in the event of the private market drying up. The congressman looked unconvinced.

Government election cycles – in New Zealand as in the United States – do not always fit with economic realities. The New Zealand general election was set for 8 November, only a few days after the US election. A year earlier we had thought the economy would not be a major election issue. This is what economic officials always prefer. Now, worries about the future of jobs and incomes were the top issue in all the political polls. Throughout October we had been meeting frequently with Michael Cullen. Treasury Secretary John Whitehead and I had convinced him that, given the crisis, we also needed to keep in contact with John Key and Bill English. As we had when the Retail Deposit Guarantee Scheme was announced, we briefed them a number of times during the crisis. Done carefully and properly, we let the Minister know about the briefing but did not divulge what was said. While the politicians were on election footing and at war in the media, none tried to take advantage of the economic situation, nor did they misuse these meetings.

This was a problematic constitutional issue. The election date had been announced and Parliament had been prorogued. There was no formal legislative body in place to debate the issues. Following the establishment of the guarantee, John Whitehead and I received flak from certain lobbying organisations about the process. The scheme had been put in place under the Public Finance Act, which gives the Minister extraordinary powers to commit public funds, in the form of guarantees, to use in a crisis. In my mind this was just such a crisis. One lobbyist committed to small government argued that John and I should properly have gone to the governor-general and asked him to recall

Parliament. We took careful legal advice on this, which confirmed our own view – it was not the role of officials to make such a move and the Minister's legal powers legitimised the steps taken. To be careful, we had documented all meetings and decisions meticulously.

Though not pleasing everyone, the rudimentary retail guarantee scheme was now in place and seemed to be working as intended. Treasury dealt with applications from concerned institutions wanting to join the scheme, and the Reserve Bank advised Treasury accordingly. The large banks thought they were being charged too much. Finance companies and building societies were worried they couldn't afford to stay out of the scheme. Fund managers argued it discriminated against funds that were technically not classified as 'deposits'. Large businesses claimed it would stop funds being raised on the commercial paper markets. In fact, the scheme *was* distortionary and costly, as we knew when we implemented it. We'd had little room to move. But it did meet its prime purpose: it stopped New Zealanders worrying about the security of their deposits in banks and finance companies.

In the weeks following its announcement, we worked on improving the scheme. We wanted to have compatibility with the equivalent Australian scheme but they were rather vague as to how theirs would work, and they kept making changes. We and our Board convinced the Finance Minister that the original announcement of a scheme that was free to smaller institutions could end up being too distortionary, with risky finance companies loading their books at the Government's expense. Indeed, there were already signs that this was happening. Consequently, on our advice the Government imposed a risk-based price for any new deposit growth, irrespective of the size of the institutions. The big banks were still not mollified, even though it was becoming clear that they we were now attracting many more deposits from the riskier finance companies.

As expected, the final design of the Australians' retail guarantee scheme, with free coverage up to a deposit cap, did end up being more attractive to banks than our scheme. But Michael Cullen resisted vigorous lobbying from the New Zealand banks to withdraw the fees from our scheme.

Another problem, one we had been flagging for some years, was that the Australasian banking system was unusually dependent on short-term foreign funding. This had been the cheapest way to raise the funds required for New Zealand mortgages, and gaining access to these funds had never been a particular problem. Now the foreign markets were drying up. Foreign institutions with money were too worried to lend it out to banks on the other side of the world. Our Australian colleagues had a plan to solve this: a *wholesale* guarantee scheme. In essence it said that, under certain conditions, the Australian Government would guarantee bank wholesale fundraising on an issue-by-issue basis. The banks would pay a fee for the service.

In principle, the big four New Zealand banks could have accessed the Australian scheme via their Australian parent banks, thus channelling funds to New Zealand. But with Australian-imposed limits to parent funding, we thought it was important for our financial system directly to assist fundraising for the New Zealand banks. Consequently we designed a similar scheme. Less of a headache than the retail scheme, it involved only banks, and we could charge a commercial fee. The New Zealand Government even stood to make money from the arrangement, though that was not its purpose. It would also prove easier to terminate this scheme once its purpose had been served.

October 2008 had been a month of muffled fear, occasional exhilaration and grinding fatigue. Once a year at the Reserve Bank we hold a markets function when traders, analysts and managers from the banks and financial operations all over Australia and New Zealand converge on our seminar room for cocktails. By long tradition, too many of them cram in, the air conditioning cannot cope, the noise level is loud and thus it continues until we politely suggest that they continue their drinking in Courtenay Place. The markets' culture is quite different from ours and their conversation is certainly not politically correct. I usually make an appearance, shake some hands, listen to some boasting, then make my excuses and leave. But this time the function was different: Simon Tyler gave his customary welcome and the beer still flowed, but the party was more like a wake. Gone was the talk about bonuses and deals, the self-confidence and optimism. Now the talk was of redundancies and losses, of colleagues who had disappeared. No one knew what would happen next. Most of the markets people are in their twenties and thirties, but even the old dogs had never seen such conditions before. The good times were over.

Wellington – home to the Reserve Bank – is small and centralised. I live in a Victorian villa on a ridge above the central business district, with stunning views over the harbour. My daily walk to work is through the leafy botanical gardens. Climbing the steep hill home at the end of the day keeps me fit – and on an even keel.

But the crisis was taking its toll on our personal lives. I do not discuss my work problems at home, partly because my venture capitalist wife has her own complex business to run and I do not want inadvertently to disclose anything confidential. Now the crisis was absorbing my every waking moment. I monitored developments late into the night. Some of our traders keep watch on market activity even in the small hours, and for a couple of days in October we were on alert the whole night.

I always have a pile of novels and biographies beside my bed, a mixture of quality literature and relaxing trash. Around this time I counted 45 unfinished books piled there. I would take one up and immediately fall asleep. But by 3 a.m. I would be awake again, tossing and turning, worrying about what was happening offshore – as were my colleagues, judging by the dark shadows under their eyes.

Feeling leaden and dispirited in the morning, I would listen, as is my custom, to the morning business report on Radio New Zealand to hear what had happened to the US dollar, where the New Zealand dollar was trading, whether the US stock markets had suffered again and what to expect when the New Zealand markets opened at 9 a.m. And once at work I would go straight to my Reuters screen to check the overnight financial data.

On 7 November I saw that the European Central Bank had cut rates by 50 basis points. This was a large cut, but the markets had expected it. The Bank of England then surprised us all by slashing rates by 150 points, from 4.5 per cent to 3 per cent, a massive cut that took rates to their lowest level since 1955. The markets were extremely jittery. The Australian Reserve Bank had also been cutting rates, more swiftly than analysts expected, and when Australia moves, the New Zealand market rates tend to move in concert. On the other hand, the markets did not seem to too affected by the forthcoming New Zealand election.

Immediately after the results of the US presidential election, the financial markets had reflected some of the 'change' euphoria until they realised that nothing had substantially changed. The equity markets turned negative again; commodity markets were also affected; and oil prices hit a new low.

With all the uncertainty, we anguished over our November *Financial Stability Report*. Its message was bad – the worst ever. We had started work on it months earlier but, as conditions deteriorated, we had rewritten it five times, each draft portraying a bleaker situation. It was something of a relief finally to publish the report on 12 November. We held a press conference in our museum, at which we acknowledged the dangerous situation overseas but stressed that the New Zealand financial system looked sound. Again, we chose our words carefully because we knew that, should the financial markets remain frozen, the New Zealand banks had only about three months' secure international funding at current lending rates. But we could not mention that. We also could not admit that we did not know what would happen next on the world's financial markets. Alongside me, Grant Spencer used the conference to announce that we were putting in place an important new emergency measure to support banking liquidity: the Term Auction Facility, intended to provide back-up term funding to the banks, secured on their own mortgages. This facility would allow the Reserve Bank to keep the banks funded if the international markets stayed hunkered down.

It was not an easy conference. One journalist tried to make something of the differences between the two main political parties' approaches to the funding crisis. Another asked whether people should be pulling money out of their bank accounts. Such reportage could be dangerous during a crisis.

Meanwhile New Zealanders had voted in a new National Party Government. As the country went to the polls on 8 November, a National victory had seemed probable, but one could not know if the win would be clear-cut or – as likely under MMP – what coalitions might be formed. In these conditions New Zealand could not afford uncertainty as to whether a government could be formed. Apart from my professional interest in policy and my personal interest in the outcome of friends standing for parliamentary seats, I am careful to stay politically neutral.

On election night my wife and I threw a party at our house. It was really a gathering of politics geeks – we invited friends who we knew were keenly interested in voting patterns but not virulently supportive of one party or another. Among the guests were John Whitehead and Arthur Grimes and their wives; like me, they had a very particular interest in the result because we would have to work with the new government. I tuned several television sets into different channels to get a range of broadcasts and commentary. I also arranged a computer to project results from the Electoral Commission website directly on to a screen, so we got detailed polling booth information at the same time as the networks. It looked like a military command centre: radio stations running, reference charts pinned to the walls, whiteboards and flip-charts to do the analysis. I suppose there was wine and hors d'oeuvres too, but I can't remember that.

In contrast to the 2005 general election, by 8 p.m. we were pretty much able to predict where the vote was going. It seemed that the results were going to deliver a stable government, and that met our concern.

On the Tuesday following the election, John Whitehead and I climbed again the marble staircase in Parliament Buildings to meet John Key and Bill English. Though the National Party had won a plurality of seats and votes, they had still to form a government and for the next fortnight we would be in a constitutional limbo, working with the caretaker government. While this caretaker government is in charge, it does not take major actions without consultation. Normally this is no problem, but this time the world was in crisis. We were careful to play things by the book.

We met Messrs Key and English in the Opposition Leader's office suite. Also present were the John Key's chief of staff, Wayne Eagleson, and his economic adviser, Grant Johnston. They wanted an up-to-date picture of the international markets and economy, and how they were affecting New Zealand. Of course Key and English were already well informed from their own market contacts and analysis. What they really needed was our assurance that there was no hidden bad economic or fiscal news, no dead rats in the cupboard. We were able to reassure them.

We all knew one another reasonably well. I had worked with Bill English when he was Minister of Finance in 1999. I was Treasury secretary then, and Winston Peters had just been pushed out of the government by Jenny Shipley. Bill English took over the position smoothly and brought a steady hand and a cautious, inquiring approach. I had been aware of John Key for longer – back in the 1980s my wife had worked with him at Elders Merchant Finance in Wellington. Then he had been a young star among financial markets traders before he progressed to bigger roles overseas. Now he sat before us, absorbing information quickly and asking tough questions about what could happen.

We had further meetings with Bill English about the Reserve Bank's range of functions, some of which he knew from his previous time as Minister but others he had not had reason to experience – payment and settlement systems, currency and liquidity management. Mainly we focused on the economy and the banks. As well as a regular briefing, we had an unpleasant report to deliver on inflation vulnerability – inflation was still at a twenty-year high. And we had an even scarier little paper on financial sector vulnerability, prompted by John Key saying, 'What if things get worse?'

The paper examined several scenarios. First, what if the international markets went into hibernation and banks continued to have trouble accessing offshore funding? This had effectively already happened. The second scenario was, what if we had a credit crunch in the New Zealand economy and companies were unable to borrow? This was looking increasingly likely. Thirdly, what happens if a good bank goes bad? Last, a completely unpalatable question, what would happen if the international financial markets lost confidence in New Zealand banks and the government? In this case, a burgeoning national debt, a downgrade by sovereign rating agencies and the New Zealand dollar plummeting would be likely. That was our nightmare. The example of Iceland had made it clear that these were not just hypothetical possibilities. We talked about each scenario and what our roles would be in the event of one occurring. More than ever, it was important for the Minister to be clear about the specific rescue powers he and the Reserve Bank would have.

John Whitehead and I also had a pleasant farewell dinner with Michael Cullen in the Treasury building. We had got on well, even during these tough times. Apart from the global financial crisis, it had been a tumultuous decade. We reminisced about the difficult years from 1999, when I was running a Treasury department that the incoming Labour Government did not much trust, the failure of Ansett Airlines back in 2001, the shocking events of 9/11, and the other ups and downs. Michael put on a brave face, but it was the end of an era.

Back in the office, staff were busy preparing the end-of-year *Monetary Policy Statement*. This is a big exercise: over a dozen staff, every scrap of data we can lay our hands on, business visits, a week of meetings, hundreds of different opinions. But this time it was especially difficult. Most macro-financial models are rather rudimentary, and they don't integrate well with the macro-economic models that we use for forecasting. (The crisis had already sparked off efforts around the world to improve macro-financial forecasting, but for the moment it appeared a Holy Grail.) When we fed the big drop in our trading partners' economic performance into our programmes, the economic models found it hard to digest. One problem was that, with the recent inflation, strong imports and bottlenecks, the model kept telling us that the New Zealand economy was still overheated. At the same time it was quite obvious that things were cooling very fast.

Overseas the bad news was spreading from financial markets to economies. The IMF had put in place emergency loans for the Ukraine, Hungary and Ireland. The Chinese had committed an unprecedented $586 billion to a stimulus package. The eurozone was officially in recession; the Europeans had put a huge stimulus package in place and their central banks had slashed their interest rates radically. American bank rescues continued and Bank of America had laid off 35,000 staff. The US automakers trumpeted their troubles loudly in Washington and were eventually rewarded with bailouts.

In Washington in mid-November, G-20 leaders met for the first time to discuss ways to deal with the crisis. In the United States, the government had approved a $20 billion rescue package for banking giant Citigroup after its shares plunged more than 60 per cent in a week. Two days later it committed a further $800 billion, of which $600 billion was to buy up mortgage-backed securities and $200 billion to unfreeze the consumer credit market. The UK Government cut VAT temporarily from 17.5 per cent to 15 per cent. The EU unveiled an economic recovery plan worth €200 billion, intended to save millions of European jobs. Then on 16 December the United States cut their key interest rate to a range of 0.00 per cent to 0.25 per cent, lower than ever before. If anyone in the market still failed to realise the extent of the crisis, this was a wake-up call.

The economic forecast in our December *Monetary Policy Statement* made grim reading, far worse than previous forecasts. We did not then know if we had hit the bottom. We had just seen a new current account deficit of 8.6 per cent, one of the worst in the OECD and a worrying percentage in these conditions. Working out what to do with the official cash rate was tricky. The benchmarking we had used in the past no longer looked reliable. It is one thing to cut rates by 25 points; it is quite another to look at a succession of big cuts. Eventually I decided to cut interest rates by 150 basis points. We had never done anything like that before.

We released the rate cut in our *Monetary Policy Statement* on 4 December. Initially the move shocked the media but the markets saw the sense in getting our high rates down as quickly as possible. This time I managed a full day of interviews and presentations; then travelled to Auckland. That evening was the Deloitte Top 200 Management Awards, a black-tie event. Hundreds of New Zealand's top executives attended. The stress of the day was catching up and I could feel the insidious beat of a migraine building. I left early and drugged myself to carry out my presentations the next morning. By the afternoon I had to cancel again.

With one son back from the States for the summer break, my wife and I had planned a restful weekend fishing with some friends in Raglan. With the help of more painkillers, I finally made it to our hired bach there. The next day my migraine was back. I spent the day in bed, curtains shut, pillow on my head, fighting the pain. The others had a wonderful day, fishing in the deep swells of the Tasman Sea. Sitting on the deck of the bach, watching the sun slide into the sea, I did at least get to enjoy the results of their labours.

It had been a hell of a year. But, so far, we had survived. And it came as a very pleasant surprise to be named, by the *New Zealand Herald*, 'Business Leader of the Year'.

CHAPTER 6

From Hong Kong to Basel
December 2008–January 2009

By the end of 2008 the recession was starting to bite. The New Zealand economy had already been contracting for a year, following the drought in 2007. Now, with the drought long over, we were caught up in world recession.

New Zealanders started to feel poorer. In this country our most common major asset is the family home. Roughly 20 per cent of households have other property investments, but we do not have large investments in financial institutions or stocks and shares. As house prices fell, most Kiwis saw their wealth decrease and, by early 2009, New Zealand households were significantly poorer on paper than they had been at the height of the property boom two years earlier.

Additionally, too many households were weighed down by large mortgages and having to make heavy debt-servicing payments. This had been worrying us for some years at the Reserve Bank and I had warned against it in speeches, which may have persuaded some people not to over-borrow. Our reprimand to the banks about over-lending to risky borrowers also made a difference. Still, about 10 per cent of New Zealand households – mainly younger couples who had recently entered the housing market – were making mortgage repayments of more than 40 per cent of their incomes.

To make matters worse, people were starting to worry about their job security. An opinion survey revealed that a large number of businesses were expecting to shed staff in the following three months. This was especially alarming for those weighed down with big mortgages, who stopped spending on all but essentials, in turn hurting retailers.

If things were looking bad for New Zealanders, they were much worse overseas. In the United States, house prices were falling further and faster. American households did have significant investments in stocks and shares and they too were dropping. Unemployment was at 7.7 per cent in January 2009, and rising sharply.

It was time to take stock. In only five months we had reversed the interest rate increases of the previous five years. The OCR was at 5 per cent, but we knew we might have to cut it further. We had made special liquidity available to the banks and they were gearing up to use it. The new government was considering various other stimulatory measures. Our overall strategy was to keep New Zealand markets calm, ensure they stayed out of the international headlines and to prepare New Zealanders for bad news ahead.

In the meantime, we hoped to see businesses responding to our interest rate cuts by cutting their prices and thereby easing the pressures on inflation. This was not occurring so, in a speech to the Wellington Chamber of Commerce on 10 December, I shone a spotlight on some of the recalcitrant players. Inflation was still too high and we needed to reduce it across the board if we were going to continue easing monetary policy and help the economy to recover. I deliberately pointed the finger at industries that seemed to think they were immune from world recession:

> We would hope that the electricity industry does not take advantage of its market position and keep increasing rates, that local authorities realise they need to set rates increases below inflation for a change, that the construction materials industry respond to much weaker demand, that the food industry react to lower international commodity prices with price cuts, that petrol companies keep cutting forecourt prices, that the transport industry pass on fuel price cuts, and that the banks pass on interest rate cuts. Only then will all these firms be playing their proper role in New Zealand's recovery.

That stirred up a few hornets. I was described as hawkish, simplistic and whistling in the wind, but also 'right on the money' by those who were frustrated with industries who would not assist the common cause. You can never predict or control the response to talks like this, but it was useful to bring these activities to the attention of the media.

When it came to reporting on the crisis, generally we were pleased with the news coverage. Had media put undue focus on bank vulnerability they could have alarmed depositors. Our head of communications, Mike Hannah, was constantly fielding queries from journalists. Were finance companies in trouble? Could the banks fail? Would the government support them? While ensuring media understood our responses, he kept an ear out for unhelpful rumours that could provoke panic.

We were also deluged with letters, emails and phone calls from the general public, often from older people worried about the lower interest income they were getting from their deposits and investments as the OCR reduced and concerned about whether their savings were safe. Some people, especially the elderly in this position, were angry. They didn't like losing income or the uncertainty of the times. They felt that, in some ill-defined way, the government should be looking after them better. Some correspondence was quite pointed, accusing me personally of negligence. There was little we could do about their complaints, but it was useful to have feedback on what the public concerns were. We were doing all we could to keep the system healthy.

The Reserve Bank had at that point a staff of 220. Everyone was affected by the crisis to some degree. Like the general public, individuals responded differently. There is no such thing as a stereotypical central banker – we have uniformed security guards, T-shirted IT specialists, casually dressed young economists, older bank regulators in suits. They come from different backgrounds and react in different ways to stress. Some thrive on it, some pass it on – others go quiet. A crisis can be a valuable bonding and learning experience, but it is sometimes hard to appreciate that in the middle of the vortex. We did our best to keep everyone in touch with developments. We held special staff meetings where we invited staff members from the coal face to share their experiences. These meetings were well attended – everyone knew that something extraordinary was happening. Some had partners who had lost their jobs – we tried to keep a special eye on these people.

On the other hand, because none of our younger economists had ever seen a crisis like this before, some were intellectually excited by the challenges of extreme circumstances. But they faced a technical problem. Economic forecasting models are based on normal ranges of behaviour by householders who consume, businesses which invest and governments that regulate. But normality had been turned upside down. Risk had become extreme, prices had moved unusually, behaviour had changed, statistical data had become unreliable. Could we rely on our traditional forecasting models? To make matters worse, our main econometric model was reaching the end of its useful life and our research team was ready to introduce a model that looked at the economy in quite a different way. We decided it was too risky to bring this in during the crisis – we would have to soldier on with the tried and tested.

My day-to-day worry was less with the forecasting models and more with operations. Something unusual was happening with our payments and settlement systems. We had been modernising our system, building new software applications on top of our established programmes. They worked well when tested but, unaccountably, as transaction pressures built up, the system could crash. When this happened in Wellington we had to switch to our recovery site in Auckland until we could get things up and running again. Huge wholesale electronic payments are cleared through our Exchange Settlement Account System daily. It is the job of chief financial officer Mike Wolyncewicz and payment and settlement services chief Adrienne Barlow to keep the system going. They also had to manage the extra stress on their teams late at night, when nasty international events like the demise of Lehman Brothers sent huge international financial flows jamming through the payment systems.

Normally we would take a problem at one site in our stride but, in this climate, everything mattered more. To make things worse, several of the big clearing banks had other, unrelated computer problems. Rumours started flying around: 'Bank X is withholding payments – it must be in trouble; bank Y is over-exposed to it.' These rumours were mainly rubbish but they had to be handled carefully because they could trigger runs on banks or hurt the reputation of New Zealand credit on international markets. Several times we had to alert bank chief executives who seemed to be unaware of technical problems in their own systems.

Toby Fiennes's group of bank and finance company regulators were also hard at it. With the deposit guarantee schemes we had to watch this sector closely. People were getting tired and we had to recruit temporary staff to keep up with the workload; but the redundancies in the market made finding good staff easier. Finance companies that had been operating on the edge were now rushing to get under the scheme's umbrella. Our regulators had an exacting task assessing the books of each one to advise Treasury whether they met the requirements. If we were too tough, it could mean death to the company; if we were too loose, it could mean a costly bailout for the taxpayer.

Our relationship with the big banks was changing. We do not always agree on regulation but, though we argue over bank outsourcing, local incorporation and other technical issues, we maintain good professional relationships – at arm's length. Now we needed to get closer to them – but not too close. While the crisis meant we had to work together for New Zealand Inc., we did not want banks to become too dependent on us. The banks themselves wanted to tell us what they saw in the market, what it meant for them and what they thought we should do about it. The general message from each was that their own bank was surviving, but we should worry about the others.

We kept an eye on one area in particular. All four main banks had new, foreign (mainly Australian) CEOs, largely untested in the role, some with little acquaintance with the New Zealand market. (I was pleased, though, that the boards of the subsidiaries now had more depth than previously.) They were keeping in close contact with their Australian parents – desirable in conditions where we could become more dependent on them for funding. However, we were all wary of the potential for tension between the New Zealand subsidiaries and their parents in a worsening situation.

During the crisis we stayed close to the financial markets as well as the banks. For this, we relied on our financial markets dealing team under Simon Tyler. We needed top market intelligence. At the best of times, 'market intelligence' is a mixture of rumour, gossip and fact. Now rumours were flying all over the place, denied and counter-denied until fresh news came along. The markets for their part were exceedingly worried and wanted to talk. They knew and trusted Simon. The chief financial officers and treasurers in the banks were saying, 'We can't get money in the international commercial paper markets; they're closed. It's never happened before in our lives – what are we going to do?' Simon reports to Grant Spencer who, as deputy governor and head of financial stability, keeps the big picture in mind. Together they focused on ways to get liquidity into the markets when they were in danger of drying up, and they advised me on the right times to take action.

A key scheme they devised involved residential mortgage-backed securities, where banks package up their housing mortgages in a way that allows the Reserve Bank to take them as security. For the banks, it's a short-term solution, rather like kidney patients going to a clinic for dialysis: they come in, we hook them up to the machine and pump liquidity through them, it cleans them out and they go away feeling better. But it is not a long-term solution and introducing the scheme was not a straightforward decision – securitisation had been tarnished as one of the contributors to the crisis, after all. But after much analysis, in December 2008 we went ahead.

We have a small team of half a dozen led by John Groom who look after domestic markets, ensuring they have enough money to run smoothly overnight. Because large amounts of funds may come and go through the banking system in a very small space of time, we inject or remove money on a short-term basis so that the banks have liquidity when they need it. Now we found it hard to keep the cash balances up to target – the banks were refusing to lend to one another. They knew it would cost them more holding on to large cash balances overnight, but they felt safer retaining the money. That meant that the next bank along the line would be short of cash. John and his team monitored the cash flows carefully. Several times they needed permission to raise our management limits, allowing them to put in extra funds. The overnight markets gradually calmed down.

David Drage leads our financial markets intelligence team. Like Simon, he was keeping in touch with the financial traders, talking to them early in the morning and late at night, hearing their complaints and rumours and worries, filtering and translating their gossip. Their language is full of military analogies. They speak of 'carnage on the battlefields' and 'blood running through the gutters'. Market players can be narrow in their outlook and very fickle. One day they are over the moon; the next day everything is a disaster. And, like the bankers, they want to share their worries. During this period we would hear from time to time that another one had been made redundant. Perhaps they had been paid a huge bonus last year, but nothing this year – and next year they might not have a job.

Our traders had a particularly hard role. Our risk unit would say, 'Yesterday you dealt with institution X, now there are all these rumours about it. We had an exposure of $250 million two days ago, now get it down to zero – get out of those positions.' At the same time, everybody around the world was trying to cash up similarly. I would see an announcement about a particular overseas institution come up on my Reuters screen and I'd ask, 'Do we have any exposure to them?' Often the response would be: we used to, but we managed to get out in time. But as one of our team warned me, 'It hasn't happened yet, but one day, Alan, we're going to come back to you and say that we have just had an overseas counterparty default.'

We were making much lower trading returns now because we were doing what every other institution was doing – dumping risky instruments and searching for quality. We were trying to put money in triple-A sovereign investments (foreign governments with the highest ratings), but they were offering lower and lower returns as everybody else wanted to put their money there too. In mid-December 2008 the return on US three-month Treasury bonds, usually the safest short-term money in the world, actually went negative. Had we invested in them, not only would we have received no returns, *we* would have had to pay *them*. That extraordinary situation (it last happened in 1929) showed just how topsy-turvy the markets were, and how hard it was to know where to invest.

Through 2007 and much of 2008, New Zealand exporters had been struggling with the high New Zealand dollar. (It had been high partly because we had been getting such good commodity prices, partly because of the pre-crisis appetite for risk in global investments, and also because of our high interest rates.) During 2007, we had intervened in the FX markets, selling New Zealand dollars and buying foreign currency, aiming to knock the top off the New Zealand dollar. Building up our non-borrowed foreign reserves would also enable us to intervene more effectively if the New Zealand dollar needed support in future. It was a risky manoeuvre, but we were taking a long-term view.

Our interventions appeared to have been quite successful in making it clear to speculators that they did not have a one-way bet. Then, as the crisis bit deeper, there was a worldwide move back to the US dollar, seen as the safest reserve currency, and the New Zealand dollar dropped rapidly, from a peak of US81 cents to 53 cents by the end of 2008. We watched anxiously. We could be making heaps of money – in four months our unrealised position had grown in value by almost $1 billion by holding more of our foreign currency reserves in an unhedged (open) position. But the markets were volatile. Over Christmas the New Zealand dollar rebounded, the rally reducing our windfall somewhat. But in the new year the currency fell strongly and during the month of January it dropped a further ten cents.

We were still making money, but our concerns had undergone a complete about-face. We were increasingly worried that the New Zealand dollar might fall too far. We feared most the possibility that global chaos could cause the market for the New Zealand dollar to dry up altogether – in which case the Reserve Bank would have to become a market-maker of last resort. The New Zealand dollar continued to drop until, on 2 March 2009, it hit US49 cents. We wondered how much further it could go.

The answer did not lie in our hands. All depended on the crucial Northern Hemisphere financial markets and their governments' efforts to stimulate them. To hear first-hand how my overseas colleagues were managing, I attended the Financial Stability Forum in Hong Kong in December 2008.

It was a quick trip – two nights in the air and one on the ground. New Zealanders are used to long-distance trips, the disorientating time changes and the jet lag that hits on return. Air New Zealand lounges, business class lie-flat seats and BlackBerry phones have made such trips easier for me. Usually I board the plane, put on headphones, study my meeting notes, read reports and reflect on the challenges to come. Then I turn on a bad movie and take a sleeping pill.

Held in an ornate but soulless hotel ballroom in Hong Kong, the Forum brought together bank and securities regulators, central banks and treasuries. We started with a crisis update from John Lipsky, the IMF deputy managing director. From his desk in Washington DC he was beamed in by video to a giant screen at one end of the ballroom. At 6 foot 6, Lipsky is a big man, genial and well-informed. His visage dominated the room, his lined face revealing tension and fatigue. He told us that he hoped the global financial system had moved back from the brink of chaos, propped up by the huge provisions of liquidity, government guarantees, and looser monetary and fiscal policy. But he warned that trouble could still lie ahead, global assets could spiral downward and liquidity could dry up. Anxious discussion followed his presentation. When I glanced up at the screen again, Lipsky, in full view, had nodded off to sleep. We all felt sympathetic: it was 3.30 a.m. in Washington!

I heard worrisome stories about events in the Northern Hemisphere from some very fatigued central bank regulators. A common complaint was the lack of communication. Some European regulators were annoyed that they hadn't heard about the big bank failures from other regulators. Others were upset about the Irish and the Icelanders, who had frozen their banks' funds without much international discussion. Yet international financial cooperation was wider spread and more complex than it was in the 1920s, for example, when it was in the hands of a small club of central bankers in the United States and Europe. This

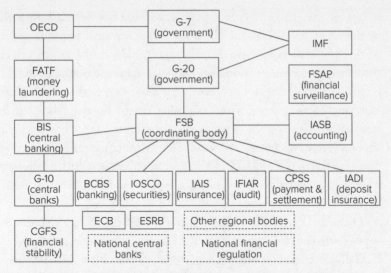

The complicated network of international financial regulators. This (vastly simplified!) diagram shows the complexity of international regulation, including the most important regulatory bodies and standard-setting agencies. Developed from 'The Financial Crisis: Whodunnit?', talk by Howard Davies, August 2009, available at www.rbnz.govt.nz.

time there was a confusing alphabet soup of bodies with interlocking responsibilities: IOSCO, BCBS, IASB, G-20, FSF, IMF.* Though effective communication had fallen short, all agreed it was vital.

Many of the regulators' complaints were understandable. They wanted more transparency, appropriate regulation of how loans originated and were distributed, control over incentives to brokers and banks, and closer oversight of credit rating agencies and investment banks. Actions taken by one country – even a tiny one like Iceland – had sparked international repercussions.

But already proposals to address the problems were being picked apart by individual countries, whose politicians wanted to attribute

---

* IOSCO – International Organization of Securities Commissions; BCBS – Basel Committee on Banking Supervision; IASB – International Accounting Standards Board; G-20 – Group of Twenty Finance Ministers and Central Bank Governors; FSF – Financial Stability Forum; IMF – International Monetary Fund.

blame for the crisis and ensure that they would not be disadvantaged in the clean up. When the chips are down, national interests come to the fore and, as happened in the 1930s, individual countries were considering adopting nationalistic policies, taking actions that might be good for them but not necessarily for the region or the world. Most worryingly, some countries were imposing 'beggar-thy-neighbour' trade restrictions. This was the slippery slope that in the 1930s had brought about a severe contraction in world trade. Most of the trade-restricting measures put in place so far did not directly affect New Zealand, but we were alarmed when we heard of price support and incentives for dairy farmers in the EU and the US.

I came back from Hong Kong with the view that New Zealand was coping with the crisis better than many countries, but that our recovery crucially depended on the international responses. New Zealand was a cork tossed in global oceans. The best we could hope for was to keep the waters around us as calm as possible.

Back in Wellington we had our final Board meeting of 2008. Minister Bill English attended and we signed, with some ceremony, a new Policy Targets Agreement. With the markets in disarray, I had not wanted to make alterations to the agreement that would add to uncertainty. The Minister agreed. In our new version, the government slightly restated its own objectives but the rest of the text was unchanged. We issued a low-key press release, and made sure we didn't have a repeat of the last renegotiation, years earlier, when the Reserve Bank reported that I had 're-signed' the agreement and rumour flitted around the markets that I had 'resigned'!

I had stepped off the plane from Hong Kong just in time to attend the staff Christmas lunch. Once a year we invite everyone, in two sittings, to the staff canteen, where senior managers serve up a traditional Christmas dinner – turkey, potatoes, carrots, greens and gravy, with healthier options. I was too jaded to enjoy the feast but it was good to catch up with employees. I asked one woman what she thought Santa might be bringing her this year. She looked downcast and said, 'Nothing.' It turned out that her builder husband had been laid off and, with no prospect of work, they had agreed to give no presents that year.

There was more to do before year-end. We sorted out responsibilities for monitoring the markets over the break and identified companies that might have trouble meeting year-end balance dates. Finally I turned off my computer, filled my briefcase with unread papers and thankfully locked the door of my office for the year.

Our two sons were both home from their American universities. After a quiet family Christmas at home we drove out of Wellington to our forest retreat in the Tararua Range. Christmas is the only time I can catch up on serious reading and this of all years I was behind. I had borrowed from the public library two biographies of Franklin Delano Roosevelt and a couple of books on the Great Depression – admittedly not everybody's taste in holiday reading.

I didn't think that we were heading into a depression but I did want to compare the events. Even today, economists disagree about what caused the Depression, why it continued and how it spread from one country to another. At various times regulators and policymakers thought they had cured the economic problems, only to see them pop up again. It ended definitively only with the massive expenditure of World War II. The towering figure of the period was Franklin Delano Roosevelt. From being a lightweight playboy, he was elected to office in 1932 as a fiscal conservative, pledged to balance the budget, then changed his approach. Maturing rapidly in office, he gained gravitas and put in place radical policy measures to fire up the economy. Some of these measures live on.

Over Christmas, whenever the cloud cleared and the transmitter on the distant hill was in sight, I kept in touch with colleagues by cellphone. There seemed to be no particular market interest in the Kiwi dollar or other New Zealand markets. Even the international markets were quiet. Nobody was taking risks. It was as though everybody was exhausted and had gone home and shut the door.

I returned to work reinvigorated, if not completely confident. About half the staff was back at work – far more than usual – reflecting their commitment and interest. We wanted to be ready for the events of the next month.

On 6 January, US President-elect Barack Obama pronounced the American economy 'very sick'. In inspiring rhetoric which reached back to Kennedy's 'ask not what your country can do for you' inaugural address, he stressed the difficulties of the current situation. 'Economists from across the political spectrum agree that if we don't act swiftly and boldly, we could see a much deeper economic downturn that could lead to double-digit unemployment and the American dream slipping further and further out of reach,' Mr Obama said. On 8 January he urged Congress to act swiftly and pass his stimulus bill.

At the end of the week, while most New Zealanders were still enjoying barbeques at the beach, I repacked my suitcase and headed back to the airport. This time I was bound for a forum at the Bank for International Settlements (BIS) in Basel, another two-nights-in-the-air, two-days-on-the-ground trip. Travelling from one side of the world to the other, mid-summer to mid-winter, in the unhealthy air of a long-distance plane brings a high risk of catching a cold or flu, especially when one is feeling stressed. I could not afford to get sick.

I landed at Zurich on a foggy winter's morning and drove through sleeping Swiss villages down the Rhine to Basel. The medieval city, covered in ice and snow, glistened in the sun as the day cleared. With some hours to pass before my meetings, I took a tram out into the suburbs and hiked up into the hills of Arlesheim with beautiful views over the Vosges in France to one side and the Black Forest of Germany to the other.

The Bank for International Settlements is an important institution, acting as a sort of central bank for central banks. Set up in 1930, originally to facilitate German World War I reparations, it has had a chequered history but today offers modern banking services and provides a forum for central bankers. Outside its modern, cylindrical building, clusters of journalists huddled on the veranda, hoping to intercept central bank governors as they arrived from the Hilton Hotel across the road.

The meetings were fascinating. I convened one where the central bank governors of ten small open economies like New Zealand got together. Our experiences can often be quite different from those of the big countries. This time conversation was dominated by the Icelandic saga. I knew David Oddsson, chairman of the Central Bank of Iceland and an ex-prime minister, reasonably well. We had occasionally talked on the phone before the main crisis struck, comparing common battles with rising currencies and carry traders. Now he told his disastrous story: a tough little country, trying to break its reliance on cod fishing, pushed out its banks like Viking raiders into European markets. The banks did spectacularly well for some years, making money from riskier and riskier positions until their difficulties rebounded on an economy that was too small to support them. The governor was under massive personal strain – while being burned in effigy at home, he had had trouble getting foreign currency to travel because the krona had become almost unconvertible. A few weeks later he was unceremoniously sacked and in a 2010 parliamentary inquiry charged with shared negligence.

The main reason I'd gone to Basel was to hear from the governors of central banks in the big economies. We sat around a huge circular table in a harshly lit room in the BIS tower building and listened to first-hand updates. The managing director of the IMF, Dominique Strauss-Kahn, spoke first. A Frenchman, he had been turning the traditionally hands-off IMF upside-down, correctly identifying the depth of the world recession and urging governments to put in place stimulatory spending and monetary policies. I listened with interest. Monetary policy is designed to be tightened or loosened in a mechanical way, but fiscal policy is another matter. Over recent decades, the tendency had been to use fiscal policy to deliver government services, not as a short-term stabilisation tool. Could governments move quickly to stimulate private consumption? Would financial markets fund it? Who would ultimately pay? And how easily could governments later cut back their spending? DSK, as he is known, did not seem too worried about the long-term issues: in his view, governments had to respond fast and aggressively.

Then we heard from individual governors. Among them was Ben Bernanke of the Federal Reserve; Jean-Claude Trichet, a cosmopolitan

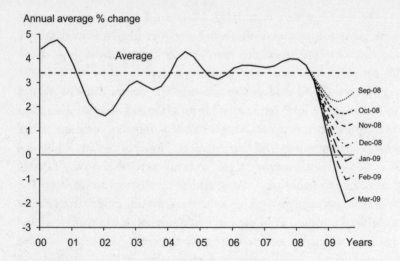

Annual average % change

Average

Sep-08
Oct-08
Nov-08
Dec-08
Jan-09
Feb-09
Mar-09

Years

How forecasts for world growth declined in 2008/09: world GDP growth, forecast twelve months ahead. Source: Consensus Inc., RBNZ estimates

and articulate Frenchman who heads the European Central Bank in Frankfurt; Mervyn King, the erudite governor of the Bank of England; Masaaki Shirakawa, the new governor of the Bank of Japan, quiet but insightful; and Zhou Xiaochuan, the tall, forthright governor of the People's Bank of China. The stress of the crisis, late nights and world travelling showed on many faces. These were the people who had to make the front-line decisions and bear primary responsibility for responding to the crisis.

Agreed convention at the Bank for International Settlements means that what is said in the room stays in the room. But the talk was as chilling as the snow outside. We heard of economies that were contracting as never before. House prices were plummeting, defaults occurring, homeowners walking away from their houses, industrial production tumbling and unemployment rising. The financial sector crisis had worked its way through the world economy. Some Eastern European and Baltic countries were recording shocking economic contractions. I heard such phrases as 'falling off a cliff' – not the sort of language central bank governors normally use.

Everyone was interested in China. After vigorous growth in 2008, China's Western markets had dried up and almost immediately a wave of Chinese factories closed in the coastal regions, sending up to 30 million displaced workers home to their villages in the gloomiest Chinese New Year for a generation. It looked like our region's growth now depended on whether the Chinese Government's unprecedented plan to spend over half a trillion US dollars on stimulating their economy would work. None of us knew the answer.

As I sat in another plane at Zurich airport, watching machines like giant triffids spray ice off the wings before a winter take-off, I thought, thankfully, that New Zealand was a backwater. But would our isolation be enough to protect us?

Several peripheral European Union countries were now suffering in a way that defined them as a group, what we called the PIIGS – Portugal, Ireland, Italy, Greece and Spain – developed countries which had been over-stimulated in the previous decade by a low euro and which had failed to tighten fiscal policy to compensate. Now the credit rating agency Standard and Poor's had put them on credit downgrade, and the markets immediately responded by demanding a premium to lend to them.

On arriving back in Wellington, I heard that Standard and Poor's had just put New Zealand on alert for 'negative outlook'. That's not the same thing as 'negative watch', nor is it an actual downgrade, but it was a sign that we had to tread very carefully. The announcement itself caused the New Zealand dollar to drop several cents.

With the world's currencies driven by international turbulence, financial markets were trying to work out where to put their money. They had been investing in the Japanese yen and the Swiss franc, causing those currencies to move uncomfortably high. The Japanese were unhappy about this because their economy was in such poor shape; they wanted to intervene to bring the yen down. Despite deep concern about the US economy, the final currency of flight was the US dollar. As it strengthened, currencies such as the New Zealand dollar automatically dropped, reflecting the fact that investors were wary of smaller currencies.

Ironically, the short-term money markets were operating better. This was wholly due to artificial resuscitation: the large central banks pumping funds into markets and countries like New Zealand and Australia guaranteeing bank borrowing. Despite the stimulus, the banks in New Zealand had gone unusually quiet.

They were no longer borrowing actively on international markets, too scared to seek funding for fear that it would not be available. Rejection by the international markets would quickly become common knowledge on the rumour mills, staining a bank's reputation. Instead, the banks were looking at parent funding and using the Reserve Bank's emergency liquidity schemes. Our main facility was the Residential Mortgage-Backed Security Scheme that allowed them to pledge securitised bundles of their mortgage loans to us as security for borrowing funds.

This scheme was not completely straightforward and bundling individual mortgage loans into a marketable form was not easy. It meant teams of lawyers, accountants and accounts officers arduously poring over individual mortgage loan files, in some cases going back decades, in order to sift the best-quality loans into groups for a credit rating. Common overseas, it was a relatively new process for New Zealand banks, and some of them had to be encouraged through it.

By the end of January 2009 we had lent out $5 billion to the banks and we could see the process was working. We were equipped to lend far more into the banking system, and it was reassuring to know that we could. As a central bank, we have a huge ability to generate New Zealand-dollar funds against appropriate security. (We do not, of course, have the same ability to generate foreign currency-denominated funds. For that, we were relying on our own foreign exchange reserves and on the currency swap arrangements we had negotiated.)

A downside of the scheme was that it distorted our own balance sheet, which over this period grew from around $22 billion to $34 billion as we lent more funds and held more securities. In itself, this was not a problem, provided that the international capital markets eventually revived and the securitisation process continued to work. Otherwise we might find ourselves holding New Zealanders' housing mortgages ourselves – hardly what we envisaged.

There was also a danger of distorting trading banks' balance sheets if this secure but costly form of funding continued too long. Both in New Zealand and across the Tasman, banks' boards of directors were meeting in urgent session, reviewing their funding options and working out what to do if the international markets stayed closed. They responded, naturally enough, by cutting back their local lending.

We were concerned about this, and so were the Australians. In fact, regulators around the world were reporting much the same thing: banks had turned from being big lenders to being super-conservative in order to safeguard their own balance sheets and to reduce their need for further capital. That was sensible enough, but we didn't want them to put their shutters up completely; we needed banks to keep lending wisely for the good of the economy. To keep abreast of the situation, we asked the banks for extra information to assist our monitoring. We wanted weekly data on their liquidity and their lending. They used to complain about the costs of complying with regulation, but now they were very cooperative.

In the meantime we were receiving a lot of flak from corporate borrowers who could not get funds and from politicians who insisted that there must be some way to keep banks lending. Over the Tasman, Australian Prime Minister Kevin Rudd was forthright in telling the banks what to do. Ministers here were more cautious. Prime Minister John Key urged the banks to continue to lend, but he also wanted to be ready if the credit squeeze continued. Should the government be prepared to lend to corporates? If things deteriorated to the point where the banks could not do their job in the economy, we could have had to play a more direct role – as we had seen occurring in the US and UK.

This was difficult territory because it could involve injecting money, using Reserve Bank and Public Finance Act powers in ways that could distort the banking industry and lead to gaming behaviours. It could also burden the taxpayer, who would ultimately have to pay the bill. We all wanted the banks to remain the main channel of lending, but we needed to investigate other ways of ensuring a flow of funds. We carefully monitored their funding, aiming to stay ahead of the curve and planning how we might respond if market conditions worsened. We also stayed particularly close to Minister Bill English as we explored options.

With the late January review coming up, we were considering how much further to cut the OCR. The banks had also cut their lending rates, but not by much. Their argument was that they do not fund directly from our short-term rate but rather on the international markets. Here the borrowing costs were exorbitant. Therefore New Zealand was not getting the full advantage of Reserve Bank rate reductions. At times it felt like we were pushing a string. Nevertheless, we were doing better than countries such as the United States where, despite massive official rate cuts, mortgages were still expensive.

Each day we anxiously scanned our screens and listened to our financial markets intelligence people. The FX markets were fragile; commodity markets down; equity markets worse than ever, not seeing any light at the end of the tunnel; and short-term money markets were operating only at depressed levels, backed by government funds. The international capital markets were indicating they might lend small amounts, short term, but only where they were fully guaranteed by governments. The Australian parent banks put some toes into this water, and got their first positive signs of funding interest.

The New Zealand subsidiary banks had not yet taken that step. Nor did they want to go offshore and get rebuffed. We considered assisting them in a couple of ways: first, by making the guarantee from the government cheaper (they still had to pay for it); and, secondly, by making a plea for key financial markets to lend to New Zealand banks. We plotted a road show.

Up until Obama's inauguration there had been various attempts by the US Treasury to put fingers in the dike, but they knew they could do little without the new president in place. The markets were waiting. Though they had listened to President Obama's inaugural speech on 20 January, it was not enough to convince them and the market plummeted again. This was a shallow and premature reaction and showed that emotion had swept aside rationality in the marketplace. President Obama had come into office at an awful time. Careful about how he talked about the economy, he made good senior economic appointments. The expectation that he could magically wave a wand and solve the crisis was ridiculous. The losses in a market that would not be placated continued to be astonishing. The market value of Citigroup, for example, had by now fallen from $258 billion to $19 billion.

My wife and I were buoyed through the hard days of January by a plan to walk the Milford Track in south-west New Zealand. For years I had heard, mainly from overseas visitors, how wonderful the tramp was, and at last we were booked to walk it with some friends. Getting fit for it had been a particular challenge – plane trips, evening meetings and urgent phone calls had played havoc with my exercise regime. But we were determined not to let anything get in our way.

We were rewarded with sleeting rain, panoramic waterfalls, lush green mosses, bird calls as I had never heard before, cheerful guides and clouds lifting for a memorable vista at the Mackinnon saddle. At the end of a long day, the noise of the generator through the bush would signal that we were coming near the comforts of a hut. Strained ligaments, hearty meals, sandflies and the towering Mitre Peak swept away worries about the crisis. But three days is not long. At Te Anau township, back in telecommunications contact, I was soon on the phone to Grant Spencer and John Whitehead, hearing the latest developments.

In Wellington on 21 January the central business district had suffered an unexpected power outage. The Reserve Bank's payment and settlement systems had quickly diverted to our Auckland backup site, so no major damage had been done. But events that we would normally take in our stride now had us on edge. Within days of returning to work, the tensions from the world market had me wired up and impatient with staff.

The markets were still turbulent. After signs of improvement overnight, the gains would drop away. Fourth-quarter results from banks and corporates in the United States, Europe and Japan showed more bad news. The IMF came out with a special economic forecast predicting that, for the first time, overall growth for developed countries in 2009 would be negative. This was seriously bad news. The crisis had now infected the world economy. It would now attack us not just through the financial markets, as in 2008, but via the commodity and export markets as well. This would not just hurt the banks, it would hit the heartland.

We could already see the impact on export prices. Dairy prices, after the huge increases of two years earlier, dropped severely from $4,000 a tonne for skim milk powder to well below $2,000. And Fonterra could no longer sell in such high volumes. Similarly, export prices for commodities such as aluminium were being battered by the global recession. Wood prices were in trouble because of the US housing recession. Our seafood market was declining as the wealthy Japanese tightened their belts. There was serious talk about layoffs. Companies could not get credit. Business confidence was in trouble.

As we prepared our own economic forecasts for the next OCR review on 29 January, we were alarmed at how much the outlook had deteriorated in only six weeks. We now forecast our trading partners, previously a source of growth, to contract by over 2 per cent. We were seriously in recession and, looking ahead, we saw few signs of recovery. Moreover, there was huge uncertainty.

Though it was not time for a quarterly *Monetary Policy Statement*, we had to cut interest rates severely. We slashed by 150 basis points, down to 3.5 per cent. Ensuring our statement communicated the right message without shocking the markets was more difficult than ever. Announcing the cut, I said:

The news coming from our trading partners is very negative. The global economy is now in recession and the outlook for international growth has been marked down considerably since our December *Monetary Policy Statement*. Globally, there has been considerable policy stimulus put in place and we expect this to help bring about a recovery in growth over time. However, there remains huge uncertainty about the timing and strength of a recovery.

The size of the cut, coming on the heels of the 150-basis-point cut in December, took the markets by surprise but they quickly concluded it was the right thing to do.

On 30 January, the day after the OCR review, I again flew to Christchurch to give the traditional speech to the Chamber of Commerce. The subject was 'Coping with global financial and economic stresses'. The Christchurch audience was looking for positive messages to start the year, but this time the only real positives were that so far, we were travelling better than the Northern Hemisphere. When I got to the crunch point of my message – 'What if things got worse?' – I struggled to offer reassurance. My speech reads: 'Lest there be any doubt, the tool-box is by no means empty. We have done a lot already and it will take some time for these actions to have their full effects, but we are entering the year well-positioned on the monetary policy, liquidity management and prudential policy front.'

Little comforted by my own words, I was back on a plane the next day, heading to the Northern Hemisphere.

CHAPTER 7

On the Tight Rope
February 2009

On the last day of January, when Aucklanders were out on Waitemata Harbour for the Anniversary Day regatta, I was sitting glumly in the Koru Lounge at Auckland Airport, which had become a sort of second home. Thumbing through my papers, I reflected on the job ahead: to travel to several world financial markets and convince them of the desirability of lending to banks in New Zealand. It was what we call a road show. I would speak to financial audiences on the New Zealand economy and banking system, and a senior Treasury person would talk about the evolving fiscal situation and the government guarantees. We had prepared carefully, taking legal advice about what we could and could not say.

We also had to be cautious about how urgent we sounded. The economy was in serious recession, the banking system was strapped for cash and the fiscal position was changing rapidly from positive to negative, yet New Zealand remained a country with sound government, good longer-term economic prospects and a hard-earned positive reputation for its institutions and laws. This would be a delicate balancing act.

Grant Spencer had been in Europe on another matter, so he covered the City of London markets, reporting a lukewarm response from banks absorbed in weightier problems. I travelled to Hong Kong with John Whitehead. We were relying on major investment banks to arrange meetings for us with the key players. We flew in on a sultry morning and were driven into Hong Kong Island. There, in huge, anonymous steel and plate-glass tower buildings, we presented our story to East Asian fund managers. We had little response from the large audiences. The investment banker who was hosting us said the reaction was positive, but it was his job to say that, and I left with my own doubts. There was not much time to compare notes because, on the evening of the same day, I was heading back to the airport and on a plane for New York.

In New York I teamed up with Peter Bushnell, deputy secretary of Treasury, for two busy days on Wall Street. We found Wall Street itself in a state of catatonic shock. Half the financial buildings seemed unoccupied. We walked through trading floors that normally would have been buzzing with noise and tension. Now they were quiet, monitors were blank and desks unoccupied. As we walked through the corridors of the once-mighty Goldman Sachs, past the expensive art on the walls and ancient Chinese ceramics in display cases, and arrived in the meeting room with its billion-dollar views of the Hudson, Staten Island and the Statue of Liberty, I tried to understand how life for these investment bankers had changed.

We gave formal PowerPoint presentations to groups from a number of the world's giant investment funds. Despite the gloom we had good attendances from senior people. I wondered whether this might be because they didn't have much else to do. They questioned us closely, particularly on the legal aspects of the government's guarantee on bank borrowing. The impression I was left with was that if they had technical concerns about the certainty or speed of repayments, we would fall into the too hard basket. It was possible that Wall Street could provide some funding for New Zealand banks, albeit at a penalty price – but if the government were to receive a credit rating downgrade, all bets would be off.

Fearing the implications of a downgrade, we visited Standard & Poor's, who had put our foreign currency rating on AA+ negative outlook in January. They told us that they were waiting for the Budget in late May to check the fiscal position. It was critical that the national debt did not worsen. As well as checking the Budget, Standard & Poor's would look at the government's external account because they had concerns about the size of the national deficit.

Although Moody's credit rating agency still rated the New Zealand sovereign foreign currency debt as AAA, we knew we were on a tight rope. A credit-rating downgrade could stop the New Zealand banks raising government-guaranteed term funding at an acceptable cost. This, in turn, could spell a harsh set of choices: running down of bank lending, increasing Reserve Bank funding or relying on parent banks funding through branches, all of which would have serious implications.

After two days in New York, I flew via Singapore to Kuala Lumpur to attend a conference at Malaysia's central bank, Bank Negara Malaysia. The flight from New York to Singapore is over nineteen hours, the longest commercial flight in the world. To allow the Boeing 777 to fly that far they have no economy class, only business class seats. After take-off the plane turns left or right, depending on which way the air streams are blowing. To my surprise, we flew back over Manhattan, then up over Scotland, passing through night then day then night again, before arriving in Singapore. A trip like this can be extremely disorienting.

The Malaysian Central Bank was celebrating its fiftieth anniversary in style. In Kuala Lumpur an escort of police outriders with sirens accompanied me from the airport to the hotel, then to the conference centre. The formal ceremonies included an evening with the Prime Minister, a commissioned musical event, lunches and dinners, as well as high-level meetings.

At the conference, which was on central banking in the twenty-first century, I heard several famous economists and fund managers, who had been in the middle of events, excoriate the banks, international financial institutions, fund managers, politicians, regulators, central banks for the crisis – pretty well everyone except themselves. The meeting of central bank governors was more useful. All the talk was about the real economy and it was almost all gloomy. The worst-case predictions of December seemed to be coming true. Massive amounts had been poured into the market by governments; these were keeping institutions afloat, but they were still moribund. Confidence was low. The United States now looked to be in its longest and deepest recession since the 1930s.

After years of loose monetary policy, some of the euro countries – especially Iceland and the PIIGS – were now in serious trouble, as high debt levels and declining competitiveness saw them come under increasing market pressure. The Irish and Icelandic economies had been shattered, the Greek economy was spiralling downwards, and the Italian, Spanish and Portuguese economies were shaky, with serious housing problems and banking stress. Eastern European and Baltic countries – Latvia, Lithuania, Hungary, Ukraine, Romania, Bulgaria and others – were also in crisis. Western European banks that had invested heavily in Eastern Europe were now feeling the pains of those markets and taking heavy losses.

And Switzerland, despite being independent of the euro, was no longer the rock of the world financial system: the Swiss franc was soaring and the economy weakening. The two biggest Swiss banks, UBS and Credit Suisse, were in strife, which was a major problem for the Swiss Government. Furthermore, many home mortgage loans to Eastern Europe and the Baltic countries had been denominated in Swiss francs. The Swiss central bank intervened in the foreign exchange markets to try and stop the Swiss franc rising and putting further pressure on the banks and the economy.

Others currencies were also trying to avoid appreciation. In the meantime, every night as the stock markets went down in the United States, the credit spreads rose, as did the US dollar – not because the US economy was in good shape but because it was in bad shape – and there was a flight to the world's final reserve currency, the US dollar.

At the conference in Kuala Lumpur we also listened to central bank governors from the world's manufacturing countries. Over the last decade the centres of manufacturing had moved from the old West to Eastern Europe, Latin America and especially East Asia. When European and American consumers stopped buying, these manufacturing countries suffered a heavy blow. With markets closing, inventories were overflowing, orders were cancelled and shiploads of merchandise lay stranded in ports. At the conference the Singaporeans, Koreans, Taiwanese and Japanese, powerhouses of productivity, reported on their fourth-quarter industrial production and GDP numbers. They were shocking – all were negative and in some cases deeply.

Several of the governors looked exhausted and others justifiably aggrieved. It was particularly galling for those countries which, hurt badly a decade earlier in the East Asian crisis, had modernised their economies and made them more robust, promoting exports and high growth and building up personal savings and government reserves. They now saw how dangerously susceptible they were to the vicissitudes of fickle Western consumption.

As in the Hong Kong and Basel meetings, there was intense interest in – and less agreement about – what was happening in China and where its economy was heading. China imported raw materials from Australia and was therefore indirectly important to New Zealand as well as to East Asia. Up to thirty million workers had now lost jobs in coastal factories as a result of the disastrous Chinese fourth quarter. That the factory closures had come at Chinese New Year made it difficult to interpret the data, because production always drops and consumption rises then. No one knew how many of the workers would return to the coast looking for jobs or stay in inland provinces. If they stayed, would they work on the farms or try to set up industry at home?

The Chinese Government was injecting money into infrastructure through direct spending, loans and tax cuts. They were also doing less conventional things – such as opening a huge number of stores in the Chinese countryside selling discounted Chinese whiteware and brownware to Chinese peasants. Their villages sometimes had no electricity or running water, but these people had savings.

Discussion at the conference turned to what recovery might look like and how long it might take. The general view was that the old world of benign imbalances was gone forever. That meant developed countries should expect slower growth; they needed to balance current accounts, generate private savings and rely less on foreign capital. East Asian countries could no longer rely on undervalued currencies and growth led by exports rather than by their own inactive consumers. Overall, there would be more government regulation and more intervention. Central banks would become more innovative, and they would

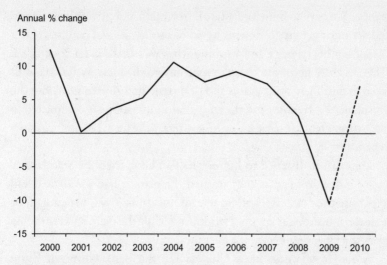

Annual % change

Global trade is hit very hard, but recovers. The graph shows world export growth with a forecast for 2010. Source: IMF

move closer to their treasuries as public funds were committed. And governments would take over more private sector risk.

We all saw that the new world was going to be different. The West would have to consume less and learn how to save; the East must learn how to consume and could no longer get away with low exchange rates and excessively high reserves. But how to get there?

I left the meeting early, on 10 February, to hurry back to New Zealand. I wanted to bring Bill English up to date on developments. I could now see that things were going to be worse than we had expected in our January forecast and they would critically weaken the fiscal situation. We needed to plan ahead.

On 10 February, just after I got back, Obama's newly appointed US Treasury secretary, Tim Geithner, announced his Financial Stability Plan. I had heard speculation about the plan in Wall Street, where everybody was worried about what it could and could not do. Geithner explained that the battle for economic recovery had to be fought on two fronts: 'We have to both jumpstart job creation and private investment, and we must get credit flowing again to businesses and families.' After explaining his strategy and warning what was at stake, he concluded, 'This is a challenge more complex than any our financial system has ever faced, requiring new programs and persistent attention to solve. But the President, the Treasury and the entire Administration are committed to see it through because we know how directly the future of our economy depends on it.'

The markets listened to him for half an hour, then the Standard & Poor's index dropped as they trashed the plan. It had too little detail to placate the markets; Wall Street did not think it was big enough or realistic; few thought it would work. And while the markets were falling away, the US Congress argued over the details.

A couple of weeks later, Chinese Central Bank Governor Zhou Xiaochuan floated the idea of making more use of international currency special drawing rights (SDRs) instead of depending on US dollars. SDRs are the Esperanto of currencies, established after the IMF was set up. They provide a reserve instrument, as their value does not fluctuate when the US dollar and other big currencies are volatile. Tim Geithner initially expressed interest in the idea; immediately the US dollar dropped. He had to rescind his comments: he had not meant to suggest that the US dollar be replaced as the reserve currency.

By February, New Zealanders have usually returned to work, rested and energised after summer holidays. This February I felt as though I had already been at work for a whole year, and the pressures were still building.

As the media went back to work and zeroed in on the economy, we had to field more inquiries from the broader public. I received many letters and emails, particularly from men. (Our surveys show that while a significant proportion of women are undecided in their views about the Reserve Bank, most men are strongly of the opinion that it is either a bad thing or a good thing.) We had letters in shaky handwriting from older people worried about their investment income earnings; typewritten letters from farmers rattled by falling commodity prices and high borrowings; emails from business people stressed about declining markets, falling profits and tough bankers – even texts from students wanting help with their assignments on the crisis. What the correspondents had in common was their apprehension about the economy and in their various ways they were looking for guidance.

I, too, appreciate support. I have a good mentor whom I talk to about leadership techniques, but he is in Auckland and, with the crisis, I had no time to consult him. But I did make a point of seeking a wide range of views. As well as taking the public's pulse from the deluge of correspondence, I arranged meetings with respected business leaders and asked them what they were hearing and expecting, and what advice they had for me. They all had strong opinions, but I was disappointed to realise that they were a little out of touch with the financial realities. They reverted quickly to defending the interests of their own particular industries, but the situation called for a broader response than just what was convenient for bankers, farmers or manufacturers.

I felt more empathy from Don Brash, my predecessor, and from colleagues in offshore central banks. Naturally, they were better placed to understand the complexities, uncertainties and contingent risks that dotted this new landscape. Donald Rumsfeld's famous observation about fighting in Afghanistan seemed apt: it was not so much the known unknowns that worried us – we could predict, model and plan for these – it was the unknown unknowns.

I kept close to and talked with my Board chairman, Dr Arthur Grimes. While the Board monitors the Bank's performance on behalf of the Minister of Finance, the members also advise me. No longer focused on inflation, they were worried about the economy and monetary policy, and also concerned about the extra assets the Reserve Bank had assumed on its balance sheet as part of our measures to aid liquidity.

I continued to talk regularly to John Whitehead and Treasury. Having been John's predecessor, I understood the problems he was facing. Treasury had to worry about the risks to the taxpayer from the bank guarantee schemes. And they had a new concern: as unemployment and social stress rose, the government was paying out more in benefits – just as unemployment and business stress were slowing tax revenue. The government accounts were under pressure at a time when the financial markets had little funding to offer. It was a tricky time for the new government to have to produce their first budget, and both John and I kept in close contact with the new Minister, Bill English.

In the Reserve Bank, we have a Senior Management Group to coordinate the different parts of the Bank but, with outside conditions worsening, I felt we needed a special Crisis Advisory Group. This was set up and headed by Bernard Hodgetts, a very experienced economist who was familiar with financial markets and provided a steady hand in a volatile time. The group met weekly and more frequently if required. Deputy Governor Grant Spencer oversaw our response to the crisis, and it was he who had to tell me if I was going astray. Don Abel coordinated operations and ensured that we heard from our currency people and those running the payment and settlement system. John McDermott, as chief economist, had the unenviable job of trying to forecast in the maelstrom. Simon Tyler attended to special liquidity measures and David Drage provided financial markets intelligence. I was comforted to have this group with their breadth and depth of experience. All (except me) had spent many years in banks and markets, they brought complementary skills and styles to the job, they were intensely loyal to me, to the Reserve Bank and to New Zealand, and I knew we could work constructively in stressful situations without any drama.

Organisational specialists say that a crisis can be a great unifying experience. We also had a great staff and we wanted them with us – but we had a lot on our minds. I had to keep reminding myself that, although the crisis had overtaken my life, I should not expect the same of everyone else. Things came to a head at the annual salary review. I was surprised some staff did not realise just how bad things were. There was general horror at the thought of a salary freeze. (I had decided not to take any remuneration increase in 2009.) We at the Reserve Bank needed to model restraint for other government departments and for the private sector, because unions and others were talking as though it was a normal year.

We ended up giving some staff very limited salary increases, but did bring back small one-off payments for people in stress situations – such as those working late at night because of the international turbulence – to reward extra efforts. We also continued to keep an eye on staff members whose private lives were affected by the recession.

Though less important in comparison to larger troubles, my own personal life was limited too. Jenny and I tried to keep up a social life but I was not home most evenings and, when I was, I just wanted to fall into bed. Even watching Super 14 rugby on television seemed too exhausting. I had taken up watercolour painting some years previously to indulge the visual side of my brain. Normally there is nothing more relaxing than sitting at one of the vantage points around Wellington's craggy coast and rough hills, painting a landscape. Now even the thought of painting was fatiguing.

To combat unemployment caused by the turmoil, Prime Minister John Key had planned a major Job Summit on Friday, 27 February. So, on a windy Thursday night, I climbed aboard another flight to Auckland. New to the job and keen on inclusion, trying to focus divergent groups on New Zealand's future, John Key had called together people from government and business, community and labour groups. I arrived early at the venue, the magnificent TelstraClear Pacific events centre in South Auckland, loosely modelled on a Samoan fale. Even at 6 a.m., preparations for a big day were under way. I had an early interview with Sean Plunket for *Morning Report*. People arrived. The auditorium had been set up with tiers of seating, looking across a stage reminiscent of the Jerry Springer set, and a real atmosphere was building up. The Prime Minister had asked John Whitehead and me, following his own introductory speech, to outline the current situation.

I told those assembled that we thought the crisis had caused the biggest destruction of global wealth – albeit some unrealised – in human history. One can argue about methodologies and whether asset bubbles ever represented true values, but in broad terms it looked like US$2 trillion had been lost by the world's financial institutions and tumbling house prices added another $4 trillion to those losses. It's hard to make these huge amounts of money meaningful to an audience. A million dollars in \$100 notes is just light enough to be handled. A billion dollars is so big it needs a very large vault to contain it. A trillion dollars is much more difficult to visualise. A trillion \$1 bills, end to end, would stretch from the earth to the sun and part-way back again. The trillions of dollars lost so far in the crisis could loop a long way around the solar system: the IMF estimated another US\$3 trillion lost through foregone production, and a strategic advisory group estimated the total cost of government rescues so far was higher than all the US intervention since World War II – far larger than the Marshall Plan, for example. And all these numbers were small alongside the fall in stock markets: equities had lost US\$30 trillion in value.

As my colleagues and I had agreed in Kuala Lumpur, the world had to change. In the deficit-riddled Western economies we needed currencies and consumption to drop and savings and exports to rise; while in the emerging East Asian economies, domestic consumption would have to rise and reserves to drop. Only by this could the world find economic balance.

I finished by saying that New Zealand's growth record, our strong employment, our flexibility, sound banking system and responsive stimulus policies should work in our favour. But, as I knew our next forecasts would be even worse, it was difficult to conclude on the very up-beat note that the Prime Minister would have liked.

After the presentation, people split into groups to discuss various issues – how New Zealand could grow faster, how capital markets could make sure of a contribution, how we could rebalance the economy and how to handle a number of social questions. I strolled around listening and putting my own oar in here and there. One aim was to generate new ideas, and the groups were certainly doing that. In reality, new economic ideas are like inventions – ten a penny – but the proportion that can stand the test of proper analysis is, like successful commercial innovations, very small indeed. The captains of industry and the leaders of the community were having a fine time coming up with headline ideas, sometimes backed by back-of-the-envelope calculations. I could see, however, that many would not pass the tests of fiscal rectitude balanced against government priorities when they were later examined in Wellington.

The working group on bank initiatives was less positive. About half a dozen bank executives were defending themselves against a very critical group of businesspeople. Unfortunately the main bank chiefs were all outsiders, three of whom had recently arrived in New Zealand, and one who had just announced he was returning to Australia. They were in a difficult position – under instructions from their head offices in Sydney and Melbourne and not able to agree to any of the proposals. I think they had sorely underestimated just how angry many New Zealand corporates were about the banking scene. As I had become acutely aware, this crisis was sparking strong emotional responses from senior people whom one would normally have thought of as consistently rational.

At midday we picked up lunch boxes and traipsed back into the auditorium for more presentations. Bill English gave a classic Minister of Finance speech, along the lines of, 'Thank you for all these great ideas, but we hardly have any money.' Nevertheless, while the technical quality of the ideas – and the ability to effect them in the current fiscal climate – was limited, John Key had successfully achieved his aim, creating a feeling of positively facing the future together.

By the middle of the afternoon, I was exhausted. Emotional extroverts tend to be invigorated by a noisy environment of people debating and arguing. Introverts like me seek time on their own to recharge their batteries. I rang my assistant and asked her to book me on an earlier flight to Wellington. Feeling only slightly guilty, I snuck away and headed for the airport.

I admit to an ulterior motive. Back in Wellington I headed for the stadium where I was just in time to catch the end of the New Zealand 20:20 cricket game against India. It's a bastardised version of cricket, but it was just what I needed. The McCullum brothers were hitting to the boundaries. After a poor middle innings, we improbably won off the last ball of the match. It was a great emotional release.

But after all the interviews and speeches, the week was not yet over. It was forecasting time at the Reserve Bank and we needed make decisions for the March *Monetary Policy Statement*. There was still a lot to ponder on, so as the stadium hubbub died down, I drove to the Reserve Bank to pick up the huge pile of papers that would dominate my weekend.

CHAPTER 8

How Bad Could This Get?
March 2009

As February 2009 turned into March and the world economy continued to worsen, we anxiously watched the stock prices. The stock market is a useful economic indicator as, despite its volatility, it signals future trends well in advance of most others. And now, by the beginning of March, the Standard & Poor's index was down by nearly 57 per cent on pre-crisis levels, its biggest decline since the 1930s. The stock market cycle was tracking the Great Depression.

In late February, the US Government coordinated the large and unwieldy regulatory agencies that jostle for space in Washington – the Treasury, the Federal Deposit Insurance Corporation, the Federal Reserve System, the Office of the Comptroller of the Currency and several other agencies – to put out a joint statement. They declared that the US Government stood behind their banking system and whatever happened, they would ensure the system maintained adequate capital and liquidity. It was the sort of statement governments make when they are really worried.

The markets must have thought the same and took little comfort. AIG had announced a loss of over $60 billion, the biggest corporate quarterly loss the United States had ever seen. The difficulties were compounded by political argument over the extra $30 billion emergency equity from the US Government, and the bonuses paid out to many of the senior executives despite the huge losses.

In mid-March in the much depressed city of London, G-20 Ministers of Finance met to prepare the ground for a leaders' meeting a fortnight later. Some political leaders had proactively seized on the G-20 as a good organisation to provide world leadership on the crisis. New Zealand is too small to sit on the G-20 – we would need at least a G-60 grouping – but Australia is a member. Through their representatives we had a chance to feed our views into the mix and they kept us well informed on developments, bringing back stories of Northern Hemisphere banks and markets in far worse shape than those in Australasia.

The G-20 Ministers of Finance had pledged to make a sustained effort to pull the world economy out of recession. The problem was that no one held a weapon, secret or otherwise, to guarantee that. The next day Ben Bernanke surprised the markets by talking guardedly of 'green shoots of recovery'. The markets mocked that they were weeds in a waste land.

The tough times ahead were acknowledged when the European Central Bank in Frankfurt cut their monetary policy rate further, to 1.25 per cent. The ECB had built a reputation as a tough inflation-targeter and initially it had looked as if the major European economies might ride out the recession better than most. No longer. Their latest rate cut pointed to a very bad situation.

At the London summit on 2 April, the G-20 leaders reached an agreement to put in place a programme of measures, costing US$1.1 trillion, to tackle the crisis. The dollar amounts were mind-blowing. At face value, this would be the world's biggest coordinated recovery package ever. But the market response was still cynical. Was this really new money? Would it actually be spent? Could it make a difference? The markets saw the package as motivated by certain leaders' political and electoral ambitions. Furthermore, they did not like what the communiqué laid out to do next. The finance ministers had promised to find ways to regulate banks, funds and trading activities so that such a crisis could not happen again; to tax financial institutions to pay for the rescue packages; and – most emotionally fraught of all – to curtail the large bonuses and other incentives that had been paid to superstar financiers, even those who had manifestly failed to maintain shareholder value.

Through this period I and my colleagues at the Reserve Bank were staying in close contact with the IMF. Together with Treasury, we share a staff member at the IMF offices and he fed us the news as their forecasts downgraded. At their headquarters in Washington the IMF had been preparing special updates of their *World Economic Outlook*. When we saw drafts, we were shocked by the numbers. Despite the introduction of substantial policy stimulus and the already considerable deterioration of global economic activity in late 2008, the world economy was expected to continue contracting sharply in early 2009. Downwards revisions to growth forecasts were widespread, including marked downwards revisions to the outlooks for those Asia-Pacific countries important for New Zealand. The other IMF publication in April was no less shocking: their *Global Financial Stability Report* on the world's financial system raised its forecasted financial write-downs caused by the crisis to US$4 trillion – half of it outside the United States. Only about a quarter of this amount had so far been written off the books in the financial sector – the rest was still to come. Would the markets be able to handle it?

Meanwhile, on 6 March a senior team from the Reserve Bank in Wellington made its three-monthly trek across Bowen Street, along the walkway above the Cenotaph, through security checks in the Beehive and across to the ornate old Parliament Building to the Select Committee meeting rooms. Here, committees of parliamentarians from across all parties routinely advise on upcoming legislation and examine public bodies on their use of public funds. We are used to appearing before them as they regularly examine our *Monetary Policy Statement*s and *Financial Stability Report*s. But this session was different. As was their duty on behalf of the taxpayer, they wanted to talk about the crisis, the steps we were taking and the costs and risks for government. The 2008-intake Finance and Expenditure Committee under the chairmanship of Craig Foss was seriously focused and prepared to put aside political differences during the crisis.

I was worried about what might happen at the session. Proceedings are on the record with journalists sitting in the back, television cameras rolling, digital recorders running and even media blogging live from the room. The Select Committees have strong powers – they can require people to attend and answer questions. I knew that I might be asked questions about exchange rates, foreign reserves, bank liquidity and a whole range of topics on which straight-forward answers could upset the financial markets. The day before the hearing I rang the chairman and explained my concern. Craig Foss has a background in financial markets; he readily understood the dangers and assured me that he would guide the Committee away from dangerous questions in public.

They treated us deferentially. (They even started calling me 'Sir'.) I sat with Deputy Governor Grant Spencer and our head of financial markets, Simon Tyler, at the front committee table, our desk almost hidden beneath microphones and recorders. In carefully moderated terms, we told them about the crisis. We explained how, partly because of the new mortgage-backed security liquidity facility, the Reserve Bank balance sheet had grown hugely to $36 billion; this had increased risk to the government, but by a very manageable amount. Then they inquired about a small company called Mascot Finance, which was in the news because it was making losses. Though a very small player, we were soon to be hearing more about it.

Since the start of the year our economic forecasting team had been struggling to keep up. As we prepared forecasts for our 12 March OCR decision, economic data continued to flood our screens, all of it bad. In addition, the financial markets were still agitated, with further bad results of banks and funds losing money, abortive attempts to raise capital and rumours of worse to come. And we were now hearing of massive losses in US heartland industrial firms. Top of the headlines were bad news stories about Chrysler, General Motors and Ford, the proud mainstays of the traditional American auto industry.

If it was hard for our team to adjust to the massive changes in numbers, it was also difficult to know how much we could rely on the old forecasting rules, the rules of thumb, the robust relationships that experienced economic forecasters use to check their stories. Many of our indicators were now showing declines far in excess of what we would see during a normal cycle. To make matters harder, we were now about to introduce our new forecasting model, called KITT (Kiwi inflation targeting technology). This new model would give us a better way of simulating household, firm and bank behaviours, including housing market developments, but first we needed to understand how to use it, how to calibrate it, where its strengths and weaknesses lay. It was a terrible time to have to iron out the kinks of a new system.

In only three months the world outlook had radically changed. We had been expecting our trading partners to grow at a rate of over 1 per cent during 2009. Now we realised that they were going to contract by 1 to 2 per cent. More alarmingly, we had thought our commodity export prices would stay roughly stable in US dollar terms: now they were forecast to fall 15 per cent. Previous forecasts of world inflation had become deflation. We incorporated these nasty international revisions into our models. Our new forecasts revealed what we already suspected: from the positive growth of around 1.5 per cent we had been expecting only a year previously, we now forecast more than a year of contraction, at maybe negative 2 per cent growth. These numbers implied that the typical Kiwi household could be up to $1000 poorer this year than if the economy had kept growing at previous typical rates, which would be felt hugely.

Our OCR now sat at 3.5 per cent, almost 5 per cent less than a year earlier. But given the wholesale rate-slashing that had taken place in the Northern Hemisphere, 3.5 per cent still looked relatively high. I considered another big reduction this time but the Committee felt that a cut to 3 per cent should be sufficient. Going further might scare the markets.

Before going public with our *Monetary Policy Statement* on Thursday, 12 March, we briefed the Prime Minister and the Minister of Finance as usual about the forecast. Bill English was intensely focused and asked searching questions. He had seen some economic forecasts and was feeling uneasy. Whereas we predicted a fragile pick-up late in 2009, other forecasters saw only worsening recession. We all knew that, if they proved right and we were wrong, New Zealand could be vulnerable to a downgrade from credit rating agencies.

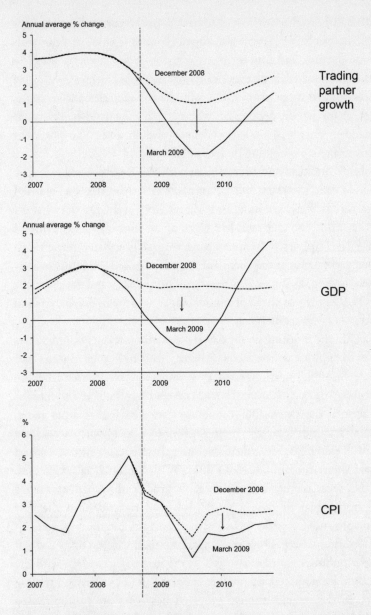

Annual average % change

Trading partner growth

December 2008

March 2009

Annual average % change

GDP

December 2008

March 2009

%

CPI

December 2008

March 2009

Our March 2009 *Monetary Policy Statement* brought some unpleasant surprises.
The graphs show the unprecedented changes to our Reserve Bank forecast for trading partner growth, New Zealand GDP and inflation that occurred between December 2008 (dotted line) and the following March. Source: RBNZ

We had hosted a visit from Moody's a month earlier. The Moody's representative, Steve Hess, is a seasoned economist who has dealt with us through thick and thin for many years. A strong advocate for New Zealand, he warned us that he could not rely on his ratings committee in New York to support his view on the New Zealand economy much longer. A lot would depend on whether New Zealand banks could persuade international markets to deliver funding, and on how prudent the government's upcoming Budget might look.

John Whitehead and I had dinner with Bill English just before the release of our *Monetary Policy Statement*. The Minister was worried where things were heading, and wanted to pose a lot of 'what if' questions. Both he and John had given up alcohol for Lent. Perhaps I should have supported them and stuck to sparkling water. But if ever I needed a stiff drink, it was then. The next day I called the Minister early in the morning, as is usual on the day of our release, and gave him the new OCR figure just ahead of announcing it to the markets analysts and media in our press conference.

Early in the morning on the day of these announcements, journalists and analysts flock to the Reserve Bank, hand over their phones and laptop telecommunications cards, then enter our lock-up where they are given copies of our *Monetary Policy Statement*. Over coffee and muffins they absorb the news. Our economists are available to brief them, but they may not leave the room until nine o'clock, when we release the OCR news. We say, 'you're live', give them back their phones and activate the telecommunications links. With the financial markets so sensitive, what used to be a gentlemanly process of journalists writing their stories had become a no-holds-barred race. Within the first minute of announcing the news, the bank analysts and the wire agencies (Reuters, Bloomberg, Dow Jones) spark up their wireless links and yell into their phones – '50! Down 50!' in the race to be the first with the headlines. Immediately the market triggers batches of booked trading orders. In the second minute, prepared headlines are transmitted – 'Could bottom 2.5 per cent. No growth this year' – followed by our full press release. Only then will journalists start giving the figures more considered analysis.

At this point I make my entry, trying not to trip on the camera cables, and address the packed room. I start by reading our prepared release which is transmitted live by webcast. On this occasion the forecast was very negative but the 50-basis-point cut was not as deep as the markets had feared. There were relatively few questions. Question time over, I returned to my office to check out the Reuters screen. The exchange rate had reacted swiftly – the New Zealand dollar gained a cent within thirty seconds.

I gave several interviews, including some by phone for Bloomberg TV in Hong Kong and CNBC TV in Singapore. In between, I slipped out for a quick stroll up to Tinakori Road, where I'm not likely to run into media: it's my way of relaxing. I had a quiet cup of coffee then browsed through a gallery before heading back to the office for more talks and pre-recorded television interviews. Finally, after a Parliamentary Select Committee hearing, it was off to the airport to catch a plane to Auckland, where I was due to give a talk at Auckland University.

My subject was the Pacific Islands, New Zealand and the world economy. For Pacific Island countries, the global recession meant lower prices for sugar, fish and other commodities, reduced remittances from the United States, Australia and New Zealand, and fewer visits by inter-national tourists. They also faced the prospect of their migrant workers abroad becoming unemployed and returning to the region to live.

We were particularly worried about Fiji which had been very hard hit, and was worsened by its political instability. The Reserve Bank governor there, Savenaca Narube, had been trying to run a credible economic policy in difficult circumstances. Commodore Bainimarama, leader of the military government, had taken over the role of Minister of Finance and had refused to devalue. The sugar industry was down, tourism was collapsing, remittances were draining and Fiji was running out of money to pay for imports. This is not directly the responsibility of a central bank, but in the small countries the governors and reserve banks are often principal sources of sensible economic intelligence and policy. New Zealand tried to help them through the South Pacific governors' network.

The Fijian governor confirmed reports about the Fijian economy collapsing and its foreign reserves draining. We assisted him to organise an emergency meeting in April in Fiji of South Pacific governors (with

Don Abel representing New Zealand). The week before the meeting Fiji had, in effect, another political coup. On 9 April a Fijian court ruled that the administration, imposed by Bainimarama when he seized power in 2006, was illegal and had to call elections. At this, Fiji President Josefa Iloilo sacked the judiciary and, as part of its measures to silence its critics, the government sent soldiers to occupy the Reserve Bank, evicted Governor Narube from his office and his house and appointed the deputy governor in his place.

We were to hear about this in snatches over the Easter weekend, then learn more details from the New Zealand Government officials group that monitors Fiji. The New Zealand Government disapproved of the political regime and its actions, so we withdrew our support for the bankers' meeting and advised other governors not to attend. We could do little for Fiji in these circumstances.

Back in Auckland on Friday, 13 March, my schedule had looked daunting. I had declined to do my usual live morning television interviews, which required getting up at 5 a.m., but I did go on Radio New Zealand's *Morning Report* and, from there, straight into a breakfast meeting to give a presentation to about 300 business people. After a few more meetings it was back on the road. Auckland's airport taxis are so expensive that I usually hire a car and drive myself. This also spares me from having to listen to taxi drivers' strong views on the economy, and when it comes to weaving my way through rush-hour traffic to catch a plane, as a born-and-bred Aucklander, I would back my own experience against that of any taxi driver.

The deadline this time was nothing to do with the crisis. It was a dinner at Te Papa, Wellington, followed by a guided tour through the touring Monet exhibition. Friends had won the dinner in a charity auction, and had kindly invited Jenny and me. Shimmering light on Le Havre harbour, textured colours on Normandy headlands, luminous reflections in Givenchy water-lilies – all seemed a long way from our current reality.

In mid-March we were due for our annual visit from the IMF. They usually send a team of half a dozen staff, hold key meetings with economic decision-makers and, at the end of the week, write a report for the IMF Board. Traditionally, they have taken a healthy but tough line about the need for price stability, fiscal discipline and market efficiency. This time was different. Coming from an institution that had been shocked by the deterioration in the economic health of the world, they were warning member countries to stimulate their economies and to do it fast. We found them gloomier than us about the world, and about New Zealand. Their advice was to cut rates further and faster. Their view of the banking world was also more pessimistic than ours. They said we should think about pushing banks to raise more capital while they still could, ahead of a worsening crisis.

The IMF review teams are drawn from economists from around the world, and sometimes we privately wonder how much they actually know about New Zealand. We couldn't doubt them this time, however, because the mission chief was not only a Kiwi but an ex-New Zealand Reserve Banker. Ray Brooks is an impressive and respected economist, and we took his advice very seriously. The team went on to warn us that the figures in the next world economic forecast from the IMF would be very bad. Reinforcing their message, the news from the other international economic agency, the Paris-based OECD, was appalling. They were forecasting a year of heavy recession: negative 4 per cent growth for the United States, United Kingdom and Europe, negative 6 per cent for Japan. The world had not seen the likes of these numbers since before World War II.

Each night brought its litany of bad news out of the States, and whenever the markets took a shock, the New Zealand dollar fell a little further. This was primarily due to a world flight to the US dollar. But we did not know where it would stop, and that was a real worry. At the beginning of March the New Zealand dollar fell below 50 US cents. But even at 49 cents there was still a well-functioning FX market. How much lower could it go before it went into a slide? And in a slide, would the Reserve Bank need to intervene to support the New Zealand dollar? We did not know.

We had started buying back New Zealand dollars to reduce our exposure to unhedged reserves, doing so covertly to avoid sparking market interest. Knowing that to support the exchange rate we might have to do this openly at some stage, we made preparations. In the meantime, there was rare pleasant news: our profits from foreign exchange trading for the 2008/09 financial year looked like they might rise significantly, a massive silver lining for the taxpayer in such a stormy year; this would help to compensate the New Zealand Government for the big falls it was seeing elsewhere, particularly from the New Zealand Superannuation Fund's losses in equities.

But this environment was hugely volatile, and nothing was guaranteed. As exchange rates and interest rates moved, we had days when our books moved as much as a hundred million dollars in either direction, giving me another reason to lie awake at night worrying about the rates.

The weak Kiwi dollar brought another benefit – it was helping our exporters remain competitive in fragile offshore markets. In addition, we could expect some improvement to our weak balance of payments position which had for a long time been the Achilles heel of our economy. Normally, a weakening currency brings inflationary pressure, through more expensive imports, but that was not a worry in these depressed times.

In the meantime, most of the banks, finance companies and building societies had piled into the Government Retail Deposit Guarantee Scheme. Knowing that they were sheltered by the taxpayer, depositors were happy to leave their funds – at least up to the scheme's deadline two years' away – in what otherwise might have been some very shaky institutions. We knew that even with the scheme, it was likely that some finance companies would fail, as some had before the global crisis. We were monitoring most of these companies and, as the property market fell, some of their lending was looking very risky. We had even constructed a death-watch league table. Therefore it was not a huge surprise to us when Mascot Finance collapsed, triggering the first claim on the Retail Deposit Guarantee Scheme.

It did seem to catch the politicians by surprise. Both the Prime Minister and Minister of Finance were unhappy about the failure, given the government's tight finances. Though we had emphasised that there was no guarantee that the scheme's safety net would *not* be called on, in hindsight the entry conditions to the guarantee scheme looked too lax. (Of course, tighter limits could have resulted in a bank run.) The failure of Mascot Finance would likely cost the government less than $20 million, a small amount in the context of our financial system. Nevertheless, this first crystallised loss, and our expectations of more to come, did not endear the new government to what they saw as the previous government's guarantee scheme.

We now looked at ways of tightening entry restrictions and putting some of the firms that had joined the guarantee scheme under closer surveillance. Scrutinising finance companies, we had found murky lending practices and very poor business models. At this stage there were half a dozen finance companies in moratorium; another half a dozen were in a very vulnerable position within the scheme's umbrella; there were also some other medium-risk firms. The latter two groups we monitored closely.

So far, the building societies and credit unions had been reporting that their deposits looked secure. Their members were loyal and their lending had been conservative and low risk. We made sure not to tar these firms with the finance company brush. Among the different types of finance companies, we found that firms lending for consumer finance and industrial plant and equipment were suffering but surviving. Those lending on property development were in chaos.

Who had been responsible for this state of affairs? Under-prepared, over-optimistic, unprincipled financiers? A gullible, under-educated investing public? Inadequately attentive regulators? An under-resourced and under-committed trustee industry? Our corrective focus was on the latter, a curious group of old established trustee firms who contract with finance companies to supervise the trust deeds under which the companies take debentures from the public. The more we examined their performance, the less impressed we were. One or two trustee firms had been particularly prominent in supervising the riskier end of the industry. We had some tough talks with these trustees, telling them the future had to be different and wanting to know how they intended to prepare. Some of them were surprised, indeed angry, at our response.

Responsibilities for regulating this industry in the future had changed and legislation passed to create a new category of financial firms – non-bank deposit-takers. From late 2008, the Reserve Bank took on the overall regulatory role, with trustees required to provide invigorated front-line supervision. Our challenge was to design a set of regulations that would offer more reassurance to investors without putting too heavy a compliance burden on finance companies. Our banking sector is heavily dominated by big Australian banks, but New Zealand needs its smaller home-grown finance companies, which provide certain services more efficiently, respond to local conditions and offer different investment opportunities. We did not expect that all finance companies should be as safe as banks – we will always need some risk-taking and entrepreneurial behaviour. Rather, we wanted to see a variety of risk/ return trade-offs that could be clearly signalled to the public.

We also knew that heavy regulatory requirements could themselves sink many of the existing companies. In the end, it was decided that finance companies would need to meet a minimum of capital ratio, get a credit rating, restrict lending to related partners and improve their governance structures. It would inevitably take several years for the surviving companies to comply and to return to profitability.

In the meantime, we agonised over whether to sort out the finance companies more actively. Many of them had significant balance sheet problems – poor-quality long-term loans coupled with weak capital structures and net cash outflows. In addition, many companies suffered from being both small and restricted to limited pools of local funding. The better companies knew this and talked to us about mergers or joint ventures to help them stabilise and grow. We were sympathetic – New Zealand needs more substantial and sophisticated financial operators. The ultimate prize that we had to offer was a banking licence, but our standards for banks are much higher than those of most finance companies and we were not prepared to lower them, especially during a crisis. We eventually concluded that it was not the place of the regulator to reposition the players on the board. The market would have to do that.

As I watched the banks, my emotions at this time swung between anxiety and irritation. The international markets were extremely fragile, but the Australian parent banks had successfully raised some short-term funding and those funds were protected by the Australian Government wholesale funds guarantee. The New Zealand Government had likewise put in place a guarantee. Further, we had gone to great lengths to educate the market about the scheme and our road show had prepared the ground for the New Zealand banks to go offshore and raise funds. Yet none of them had done so. Why not?

The banks were very apprehensive. If they were rebuffed for funding, news of their failure would instantly reverberate around the markets. The New Zealand banks preferred to reduce their loan exposures and to rely on funding from their Australian parents. We would have been more comfortable seeing less reliance on this funding channel – it could provide only temporary relief, being subject to upper limits set by the Australian Prudential Regulatory Authority (APRA).

I had been invited to a board meeting of BNZ and its parent, National Australia Bank (NAB), in Auckland on 5 March. I flew up at the end of the day, and drove for two hours through Auckland's gridlocked traffic in the pouring rain to attend their corporate dinner on the North Shore.

I had arranged to talk with the chairman of NAB before dinner. I was late – they were about to eat when I arrived – but he obligingly pulled out of dinner. We had a good discussion, encouraging each other. The market conditions were still terrible but, in contrast to the other banks, NAB had done reasonably well getting funding from overseas. They had also taken the brave decision, on both sides of the Tasman, to keep lending. As I drove back across Auckland afterwards, I reflected that their decision took guts. It was very helpful for both countries.

Australian board members who had never visited this country some- times – unhelpfully – formed their views of us based on what they heard in the Australian media. We had therefore encouraged the parent banks to hold occasional board meetings in New Zealand. They were now doing so and in these circumstances I found most of the Australian chairmen willing to discuss in practical terms what they could and could not deliver. In Australia the banks have not just a commercial but also a political relationship with their stakeholders. They were willing to have a similar relationship here too, but they were not always clear on the rules of the game in New Zealand. I had taken a rather long time to understand that. It was a classic trans-Tasman communication problem, where similarities on the surface belie significant differences, closely related as the two countries usually are.

In Wellington on 19 March it was time for our own monthly Board meeting. The crisis again dominated the meeting. How were our economic forecasts holding up? What more could we do with monetary policy? Did the banks have enough liquidity? Would the exchange rate hold up? Were we putting overly risky assets on our balance sheet? Did we foresee more big financial failures offshore? Would our payments and settlements systems keep working? We did not always have answers to the questions, but they certainly focused our minds.

That evening we held our annual Wellington cocktail party, inviting colleagues, decision-makers and people of influence to our building on the Terrace. It is one of those Wellington insider events where bankers rub shoulders with politicians, government heads and even bishops. We held the function in our museum, which allowed guests to roam around the exhibits and remind themselves about our history: we had been in crisis before. On one wall a timeline points to the disruption during the Great Depression. In a corner stands Bill Phillips' famous hydraulic model of the economy, designed for the post-war mess in the British economy. The setting could not have been better for the conversations that evening, which all focused on the crisis and its effects on everyone in the room. I introduced the senior members of the Reserve Bank as a way of explaining our diverse tasks. As usual, people wanted to use the opportunity to talk to me, some of them to good effect, some with strong opinions. I wanted to reassure them, but of course, there were things in play that I simply could not speak about.

The annual dinner with the Board and the Bank's senior managers followed. By this stage I was exhausted. Half way through the dinner I excused myself. I had to get up at 4.30 a.m. the next morning to catch the red-eye flight to Australia.

We had tough business to do there. Before the crisis we had been arguing with one particular bank about certain preparations we felt they needed to make. They had responded legalistically rather than cooperatively. Now the situation was exacerbated by world events. While many people in the local bank had been doing their best to resolve things, I wanted to speak to the parent. A colleague and I had an uncompromising message to deliver.

We took the opportunity of our visit to attend to other business. We also met with trans-Tasman regulators to discuss the global crisis. This group included representatives only from the Reserve Bank and Treasury from our side of the Tasman. The bigger and more complex western side was comprised of people from APRA, the Reserve Bank of Australia, the Australian Securities and Investment Commission, all based in Sydney, and the Australian Treasury in Canberra. They have split up their functions quite significantly, and that often led to differing views. We also had at that time a different approach to resolving bank crises.

Our approach had long been clinical and technical. When banks run into nasty situations they can quickly become life-threatening. A smaller bank is relatively straightforward to deal with, but the failure of a big bank can threaten other banks, and indeed the whole national economy. To deal with such an event, we would refer to our 'tool-kit': a long and somewhat turgid internal manual that sits squarely in the middle of the bookshelf behind my desk. But we had never had to use it in a crisis. For years we had been doing stress tests on banks: we would envisage a bad scenario for New Zealand, say an outbreak of foot-and-mouth disease followed by a breakdown in trade, with farm and house prices plummeting. A 'dark side' team of staff volunteers, playing bankers in distress, would set up in the Reserve Bank. We would then spend a day with the bad news – banks in trouble and so on – filtering out in plausible ways. Relying on our bank manual, we would devise solutions. These situation-based exercises tested how good our responses were (and they showed me whose nerves I could rely on in a crisis). But, by definition, a simulation is not real. We would go home at the end of the day with everything restored to normal.

The global crisis differed massively from the scenarios in our simulation tests. We had not envisaged a situation so bad that *all* the banks could be at risk. Nevertheless, the options in our tool-kit still offered the New Zealand Government the greatest flexibility for dealing with a crisis. If threatened by a bank closure, we could keep it open using emergency powers – or in a half-way situation we could 'close' an existing bank's operations over a weekend and 'open' a new bank on Monday morning, with the questionable assets quarantined and a guarantee on operations going forward.

Of course the Australians were making contingency plans too. Their history has been a little different from ours. Whereas the New Zealand Government had refused to bail out, for example, the Development Finance Corporation at taxpayer expense in 1989, the Australian Government had been more inclined to support their troubled institutions, such as some state-owned banks. When it comes to the big four, Australia's position is different from ours, not because the banks are more important to them than they are to us (they make up a larger proportion of our financial system than they do of Australia's) but because most of the shareholders are Australian. At the time of our meeting, the Australian regulators were anxious that that we not take action on a subsidiary in New Zealand if this would hurt the value of the parent in Australia. While we understood their concerns, it was difficult for us to give blanket assurances. Our own worry was that Australian law gives Australian creditors preference over New Zealand ones.

It was a tough meeting. Taking a strong line with colleagues and friends can be hard on all concerned. But everyone listened and the meeting did help clear the air.

It was nearing midnight as we flew into Wellington. I can always tell when we are getting close: the plane's wings start jiggling and the fuselage shuddering. Despite the hour, I drove straight to the office to pick up the inevitable piles of paper. Then in the early hours, I drove home and collapsed into bed.

It had been a desperately hard month. I had a season ticket to the rugby but had missed all the games so far. I was enrolled in a watercolour course – I had missed all the classes. The garden was a mess and the lawns needed mowing. And all I wanted to do was sleep.

CHAPTER 9

The First Green Shoots
April–June 2009

As the New Zealand summer faded and the days shortened, the world economy settled into sullen recession. The daily news was gloomy but the big shocks were fewer. It was as if the giants of the financial world had delivered their worst; now the world's economies had to digest and deal with it.

Life became a little easier for me. Reclaiming my weekends and my appetite for reading, I became engrossed in a timely new publication, *Lords of Finance: The Bankers Who Broke the World*, which recounts a period in the early twentieth century through the eyes of four contemporary central bank governors: Benjamin Strong of the Federal Reserve, Montagu Norman of the Bank of England, Emile Morceau of the Banque de France and Hjalmer Schacht of the Reichsbank. Each one was an eccentric character, a colossus with world views, personal powers and egos to match. Crises struck regularly in their post-World War I era. When bad news hit, the governors would board a cruise ship and spend a quiet week or two on the first-class decks crossing the Atlantic, updated by the occasional wireless message, arriving to gentlemanly discussions with colleagues spread over weeks – a far cry from today's stressed world of BlackBerries, airport security searches, jet planes, and real-time Reuters screens.

I read such books to try to understand the bigger historical picture. We had been so focused on the details of the financial markets over the past months, it was hard to lift our sights to the years to come. But failure to do that could mean repeating the tragic mistakes of the 1930s, mistakes that ultimately led to misery and war. I wanted to try to see this crisis from the perspective of future generations.

It was becoming apparent that the crisis was bringing about a geo-political sea-change. This was most obvious at the G-20 leaders' meeting in London on 2 April 2009. The big emerging-market countries, many still growing, were eager to show their muscle to the G-7, most of which were mired in recession.

Despite marked political and economic differences that made the meeting harder, the G-20 did reach broad agreement on a range of policies. The Chinese emerged as the major new force, promoting again the idea of new international currencies that might gradually replace the US dollar as the world reserve currency. Members pledged more money for the IMF and more issues of special drawing rights (SDRs). A new IMF facility to deliver bailout funds was also agreed upon, one designed to carry less stigma. We took a particular interest in that facility because, if things had continued to get worse, we might have need for it.

Our greatest concern was the move towards increased trade protection. There was worthy international discussion of how important it was to avoid protectionism, but this was just talk and already in conflict with what some countries were planning. A large number of protective measures had been levied by Northern Hemisphere countries on others. Outside the dairy industry, few affected New Zealand but being small, agricultural and therefore extremely vulnerable, we watched with some trepidation.

The G-20 also discussed updating the Bretton Woods Agreement, the fruit of that historic moment in July 1944 when the Allied nations met in New Hampshire to agree on the architecture that would guide international financial cooperation after the war. Its original intellectual architect was Maynard Keynes, though his blueprint was re-drawn by Harry Dexter White and blurred by the *realpolitik* of the post-war years. The framework had been revised in the 1970s and 1980s to deal with new players, floating currencies and large capital flows. Now there were calls for a Bretton Woods III to deal with the dangers posed by the giant global private institutions and their potent new financial instruments.

But for all its new-found potency, the G-20 also revealed innate weakness: there were now so many different countries around the table, with such different interests, that it was clear they would find it hard to agree on important actions once the immediate crisis faded.

Surprisingly, the financial markets welcomed the G-20 communiqué. Maybe they were impressed by its weighty talk of a new world order, or with its coordination of financial support. More cynically, they may have been relieved that it looked like another international talkfest, and felt that its threats to regulate bankers' bonuses and tax bank super profits were mere paper tigers.

After months of noisy political debate, much of it destabilising, at the end of April the US Congress offered a little more certainty for the markets when they finally approved a $3.4 trillion budget to help pay for the rescue initiatives. The IMF had just raised their own forecast of financial sector write-downs to $4 trillion.

But by now the stress had spread from banks to the old manufacturing firms of the Western world. After months of speculation, agonising and pressure from the US Government, on May Day, the traditional time for socialists to celebrate, Chrysler, one of the three great US carmakers, was put into bankruptcy. The US auto firms were facing falling demand and burgeoning financial liabilities. One month later, General Motors, the world's biggest carmaker, declared bankruptcy in a deal that involved the US Government pouring in more loans. Bondholders stood to lose up to 90 per cent of their money.

Early May saw yet more money poured into Fannie Mae after the massive mortgage-lender announced a gigantic quarterly loss of $23 billion. The continuing flow of bad news from US financial institutions was extremely damaging. In an attempt to plug it, the US Government required the country's nineteen biggest banks to undergo stress tests on their balance sheets. It was a desperate attempt to assess likely bad news to come. The Treasury said, in effect, 'Let's assume things get even

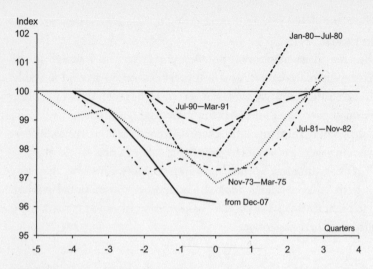

Index

worse, house prices drop even further, deposits dry up more: then how would these banks look?' On 8 May the US Treasury announced that ten of the biggest banks had failed their stress tests and needed to raise fresh capital of around $75 billion.

The continuing problems in the United States were highlighted a few weeks later when the government released its estimate of first quarter growth: the data suggested that the economy was now contracting by nearly 6 per cent on an annualised basis. This horrible figure further destabilised financial market confidence. The market mood did not lift when, a little while later, President Obama announced a major package of bank reform.

In Europe the news was no better. The amount earmarked for the UK Government asset purchase plan to buy shares in failing banks had been looking inadequate for the size of the losses, and on 7 May it was increased to £125 billion. A few months later the amount had to be increased even further. The credit ratings of the Irish Government were cut for a second time. The European Commission reviewed its forecast for the whole region and concluded that its economies would shrink by 4 per cent on average during the year and unemployment could rise to 11 per cent. Already countries such as Spain were threatened with unemployment exceeding 20 per cent, a scarily high figure and one reminiscent of those of Weimar Germany and Depression United States. The European Central Bank responded by cutting its monetary policy rate even further, to 1 per cent. In Sweden the venerable Riksbank, the oldest central bank in the world, lowered its own monetary policy rate. Astonishingly, Sweden's deposit rates were now actually negative.

Would these measures make any difference? No country was immune to the crisis. Japan announced that, despite having had very low interest rates for a long time, it had just recorded a disastrous first three months of the year: the economy was getting smaller at an annualised rate of 4 per cent, a record decline. And we heard from BP in early June that the world's consumption of oil, one of the most basic indicators of emerging market strength, had fallen for the first time in nearly two decades.

Economists cannot simply look out the window to see what the economy is doing on any given day. We use forward indicators, historical relationships and a panoply of forecasting models, but we do not know for sure how the economy is doing until we get official statistical data which comes through three to six months after the event. (Even then we cannot know precisely, because statistical agencies regularly make statistical revisions which may be big enough to change our view.)

Now, as we reviewed the data, we wondered if at last we could see the trough ahead, the point when quarterly GDP reaches its lowest level and the economy gradually starts improving again. Of course, not all aspects of the economy recover at once. Some lagging sectors, such as the labour market, would continue to worsen even after GDP started to improve.

Were we right to glimpse a turning point? On 16 April the Paris-based OECD released their forecast for New Zealand, the result of their recent fact-finding trip. It was a very negative picture of a small country in a world that would not recover for another year or two. No turning point there. The New Zealand Treasury was preparing its own forecasts for the upcoming Budget. They were also very negative, picking no growth for the year. There was little agreement among the dozen or so other private sector forecasters.

Being economists, we know that a half-filled glass is also half empty. We submit all our forecasts to a 'WIWAW' test: 'what if we are wrong?' If we were being over-optimistic and the recession still had some way to run, we would lose the opportunity to apply more monetary stimulus and potentially prolong the agonies. On the other hand, if we were being over-pessimistic, and the recovery was indeed near, our continuing loose monetary policy could feed inflation in a year or two.

However, if we were correct and recovery was in sight, there would be another reason for relief. It would mean that our highly stimulatory monetary and fiscal policies had helped – and that we would not need to apply serious emergency policies like the quantitative easing and bank bailouts that my colleagues in the Northern Hemisphere had been forced into. These unconventional policies are untested, they can be unpredictable, they invite gaming distortions and they are expensive to the taxpayer. In addition they are hard to exit, leaving market uncertainty, political pressures and fiscal scars. Already in the Northern Hemisphere we could sense a new and difficult relationship between banks and government, rife with moral hazard, sullen resistance from a taxpaying public who resented the support for bankers, huge bills looming as governments committed to support packages and nasty hangovers.

As the dire news accumulated, it was crucial for us to keep looking at the big picture. What might New Zealand's recovery look like in this new world? How would the world have changed? Where would we fit? I foresaw a trading world slanted to emerging market demand, one where New Zealand met the requirements of the growing Asian middle classes rather than just the historic requirements of US and EU markets. A financial world where things would be tougher, with less tolerance for imbalances, weakening fiscal stories, chronic debt, growing current account deficits and one-sided, property-laden balance sheets.

We argued intensely about these issues in the Reserve Bank and with senior colleagues at Treasury. We talked about how we might co-ordinate smooth exits from the various government stimulus measures.

These seemed doable and certainly easier for us than for the Northern Hemisphere countries, though the daily news from buffeting world markets warned us that it could still be a long trek.

Even if we were right in thinking that we could recover without too many scars, we still faced two particular problems. One was the likely limitations imposed by unsympathetic market conditions: high international interest rates, the legacy of a now risk-averse world, would not help our recovery. Similarly, a high exchange rate as traders reduced their US dollar holdings would make an export-driven recovery very difficult. We did not know if this scenario would eventuate, but it seemed likely.

Our second worry was that we feared returning to the old treadmill whereby, at the first signs of recovery, New Zealanders flocked back to property. This could send house prices up, with heavy mortgage borrowing financed from abroad putting further pressure on the exchange rate, which in turn could cripple the trade sector and further distort the balance of payments.

We could influence the property issues. We argued internally and with Treasury about ways to neutralise the tax advantages of property investment, about reducing the fiscal stimulus at an appropriate pace and about making the OCR more potent when necessary. We also discussed the problem with the Minister of Finance and the Prime Minister who understood our concerns completely, but were cautious about the wider implications. At the same time, taking care to preserve our political neutrality, we briefed both Government and Opposition caucuses on the crisis and the hoped-for recovery. We had very positive discussions, leaving me to wonder whether the crisis might have delivered New Zealand a rare chance for political consensus on the economy.

April brought a crisis of a different nature with the outbreak of influenza A (H1N1), a rare and potentially virulent virus in the United States and Mexico. Reporting that it originated from handling pigs, the media dubbed it 'swine flu' and told us the virus was widespread in Mexico, it hit young people hard, could be fatal and would spread fast. Any comfort we had from our geographical isolation was dissipated a few days later when we heard that there were suspected cases in Auckland, some of which were subsequently confirmed. The World Health Organization (WHO) declared a pandemic alert, raising the alert level to phase 5 at the end of April. On 11 June WHO put the world on the highest pandemic alert, phase 6.

With our traditional dependence on agriculture, New Zealand has always put biological threats high on the list of hazards. Our greatest fear has traditionally been a foot-and-mouth outbreak, because it could be disastrous to trade. A Reserve Bank foot-and-mouth simulation in 2003, based on a set of assumptions (for example, that the outbreak is contained within the North Island), modelled a likely cumulative fall in nominal GDP of 8 per cent over two years. Thankfully, this has never happened, though we have had a number of credible scares. (When these occur, the Reserve Bank is briefed so that we can inform and reassure nervous financial markets.)

We have, however, faced a number of real biohazards. Foremost among them was the SARS crisis of 2003, which hit our tourism hard for a short time, but was more damaging in East Asia. The avian influenza epidemic of 2003–04 had less economic impact. We knew that these events can provoke a run for cash, and had put plans in place to ensure that we had plenty of spare cash in our vaults and on reserve at the note-printer, and emergency procedures to keep the banks' ATM machines stocked.

But earlier events had had only a limited impact on the economy. Would swine flu be similar? It seemed to me that the threats of swine flu were being over-hyped by both media and health interests. We might see some reduction in tourism and perhaps a drop-off in demand for meat, but hopefully not much more damage than that. But with the world in crisis, we would have to take this event seriously.

As we had when SARS struck, we reviewed our cash holdings. Reserves of $5 notes were a little low, but they are not so important. We had good stocks of $20 and $50 notes, the ATM feed stock. If necessary, we could fly more cash in. That seemed satisfactory. We also installed hand-sanitising machines around the building, instructed staff on hygiene and contagion and sent people home at the first signs of illness. An analyst returning from Australia with flu-like symptoms was bundled straight home. Because babies and toddlers are particularly susceptible to infection, we made contingency plans to close down the children's crèche in our building. We restricted travel, planned to use video and phone conferencing and reduced the number of face-to-face meetings. We hunkered down.

I was due to fly out to a meeting of the Bank for International Settlements in Basel in mid-May. We monitored the swine flu risks, and I decided it was still sensible to travel, taking with me a dose of the antiviral drug Tamiflu. Over the next month we studied the potential impact of swine flu on the New Zealand economy. We were most worried about the likelihood that contagion rates could lead to a high proportion of the work force staying at home as a precaution or to look after children where schools had closed. We tracked the impacts on the labour force, on productivity, on consumption, on confidence and on potential growth. While there would be a real human cost, using reasonable assumptions, our baseline forecasts suggested a limited economic impact with declines in output of less than 0.6 per cent in the first year. This was relatively encouraging. A global flu crisis on top of a global financial crisis could turn out to be particularly ugly.

Leading up to the April 2009 review of the official cash rate, we carried out our usual visits to New Zealand firms to gauge the pulse of business. We regularly visit around sixty firms in a range of different industries across New Zealand. In this small country we are able to get an insight into a large part of our economy by direct contact and most businesses are generous with their time. Whenever I can spare mine, I accompany one of our younger economists on these visits, usually to Auckland, which is the country's economic powerhouse. Our April visits were muted, but we found some firms doing surprisingly well: a printer-packager with a very sophisticated product, a well-known transport company that had kept profitability by slashing capacity, a family firm selling sophisticated industrial electrical gear to the Australian Government, a tiny foundry claiming world leadership of a new infrastructure product. As usual, we had to address questions about the world crisis that we could not answer, and hear complaints about the government that we could not practically influence.

While there was some optimism among smaller business, a couple of our big firms were deeply troubled. These firms had been hit hard by tough trading conditions, and the state of their balance sheets was worrying. Some had been caught with unexpected foreign exchange exposures. In the space of a month, the New Zealand dollar had unexpectedly risen by 10 cents. By the end of May it had gained 15 cents. That had eaten up the profit margins of uncovered exporters. Normally manageable, the companies feared that in these fragile circumstances the markets could hit stock prices, trigger default covenants and cause financial stress.

Often in the evenings, just when I feel like going home, I have to attend cocktail parties and other events. I enjoy some of these; some are important for talking to people I might not normally meet; and other events I find rather boring but they are part of the job. On 29 April I attended two important events that marked a parting of the ways. First, in the ornate Grand Hall of Parliament Buildings, invited guests farewelled Michael Cullen from Parliament. As expected, he delivered a brilliantly witty and sardonic speech looking back over his long career. I had worked with him since his appointment as Minister of Finance in December 1999 until the Labour Party's election defeat in 2008. It had been a positive decade of growth until the final year, and I am sure Michael regretted not being in office to see New Zealand through the crisis.

But democracy can be ruthless – out with the old government and in with the new. I shook Michael's hand, left the reception and walked up Hill Street, over the motorway towards the cloud-covered Tinakori Hills and on to Premier House, the sprawling weatherboard villa that is home to New Zealand's Prime Minister. It is not particularly fancy (an earlier Prime Minister's spouse described it to me as 'just a very big state house') but downstairs there is a gracious dining room decorated with fine New Zealand art where I joined the other guests of Prime Minister John Key. The occasion was a farewell dinner for the retiring head of the Ministry of Foreign Affairs, Simon Murdoch. Simon had been an eminent mandarin, adviser to many ministers and prime ministers, and it was a nice touch for John Key to host this dinner. We had some pleasant New Zealand food and wine. Conversation was light and varied, but the topic of how New Zealand could survive the crisis was never far from the surface.

At the end of April our analysts were hard at it again, putting together economic and financial forecasts for the upcoming OCR review and our *Financial Stability Report* shortly after. Our forecasts now showed the worst picture of the world economy that we had ever seen. The changes in data were so great that it was hard to put them in perspective. Could we really be seeing such sudden contraction? Could we trust our models? Would the cash rate change have the expected effect?

The forecasts showed the New Zealand economy was likely to keep contracting for perhaps a year and a half to two years, causing a recession not seen for a generation. Only then would we move towards a fragile recovery and we hardly dared to speculate what it might look like. For the first time as an economist, I started seriously to wonder about just how tenuous our Western market-based world might be.

Mindful of the gravity, the OCR Advisory Group sat around the long mahogany table in the boardroom. On one wall hangs the Reserve Bank royal crest proclaiming *securitas et vigilantia*. The other side of the room is businesslike, a screen where we project graphs and models, a whiteboard and the ubiquitous trolley of tea and coffee to keep members awake. But there was no difficulty invigorating the group on this occasion. Our official cash rate was 3 per cent. It was already having an effect: mortgage rates had dropped, but by only a little, reflecting the higher cost of international funds. Kiwis' love of term mortgages meant that most mortgage holders would have to wait a year or more to see the lower rates.

It was clear interest rates needed to be cut further. But how far? We were in uncharted territory. We had watched the old G-3 economies (the eurozone, Japan and the United States) cut rates to near zero, but we did not think that was a practical option, given our need for an interest rate positive enough to attract foreign funding of our deficit.

I concluded that we could comfortably cut our OCR to as low as 2 per cent. Below that might be dangerous. But, after more than the usual amount of argument, I decided to cut rates to 2.5 per cent. If there had been enough support around the table we might have gone a little further, but this was no time for dissent. I did not think it appropriate to overrule the majority view.

We had other problems: despite our urgent need to get rates down, the international markets were actually pushing up long-term interest rates. This was partly because nervous markets were demanding high-risk premiums for lending, but also because markets realised that the colossal fiscal deficits the OECD countries had built up over recent months would have to be funded by borrowing. In addition, financial markets were speculating about fiscal-fuelled inflation threats, and were starting to build in an expectation of monetary tightening in years ahead. We desperately wanted the price of money to come down, but it was resisting our efforts.

The Swedish Riksbank and the Bank of Canada, facing similar problems, had tried an unorthodox solution: they cut rates and assured markets that the rates would not rise for a long time. We decided to try this but, given the sensitivity of markets (they analyse our releases in detail, poring over every adjective and subordinate clause for nuances) we had to do it with care. Every quarter before we put out a press release, we test various sets of hawkish and dovish terms about monetary policy. This time we had a new phrase in our press release: 'We expect to keep the OCR at or below the current level through until the latter part of 2010.' In central banking terms this was an unusual commitment.

The markets digested the message, then shook their collective heads. The 90-day interest rate track moved down but not by much. Long-term rates remained stubbornly high. Markets did not find our promise particularly credible. And we waited for the banks to drop their interest

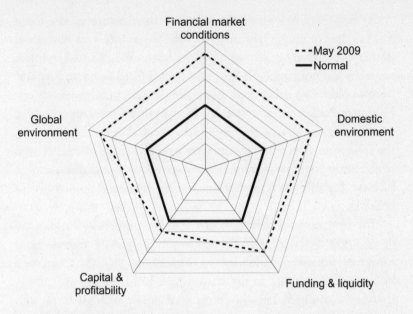

Financial market conditions

--- May 2009
— Normal

Global environment

Domestic environment

Capital & profitability

Funding & liquidity

Our financial stability cobweb – measuring the extent of financial instability in New Zealand during the crisis – looks very unsteady. The further along each axis from the centre, the more unstable the economy. For details of how this is measured, see the Reserve Bank's Financial Stability Reports, available at www.rbnz.govt.nz.

rates, reflecting our 50-basis-point cut, but they didn't budge. Kiwibank, government-owned and a relative newcomer, had been leading the way with competitive interest rate cuts over the preceding year. Now that their capacity to lend had slowed, they were sitting on their rates. The other banks showed no signs of moving, presumably delighted at the prospect of recouping their narrowing lending margins.

A fortnight after the OCR we were back in front of the media presenting our May *Financial Stability Report*. I had been dreading it. In my time we had never had to deliver such a grim message. The report stated that New Zealand finance companies were in disarray and our bank funding and liquidity were fragile, but that the system was holding up – so far. I feared what the financial media might do with this. In these fragile times a single headline like 'Reserve Bank fears for stability' could have started a bank run.

As had recently become the norm for these occasions, the room was full, but to my surprise and relief the journalists were restrained. Rather than ask about the safety of the banks, they wanted to know why they had not passed on any of the latest official cash rate cuts, and what would we do about it. So also asked the Select Committee at our hearing in Parliament later that day. Parliamentarians are very sensitive to the public mood, typically more so than central bankers. Members at the table from all political parties were strongly critical of the decision by the banks not to pass on interest rate cuts. A deep-seated resentment by New Zealand mortgage-holders and New Zealand businesses was building.

The New Zealand business sector had been suffering. Profits were down across the board, staff lay-offs were in progress, investment had halted and firms were finding it hard to get funding. This was worsened by the banks' response to the crisis, which had been to cut lending, abandon committed lines of credit and impose onerous terms and conditions on banking covenants. Businesses argued with local bank managers, who in turn blamed policies imposed by Australian risk committees. We heard from many businesses. Some were under real pressure, and there was a rising tide of anger towards the banks, not just from smaller fringe firms but also from large blue chip companies.

Banking relationships that had been built up over decades did not seem to count for much. I had an extraordinary conversation with one very well known company where the chief financial officer vowed to get even with his bank, no matter how long it took. The banks, focused as they were on their own problems of funding, seemed surprisingly unaware of this mounting opinion. Regardless of the benefits Australian banks in New Zealand have received in the past and the committed assistance in the form of guarantees and liquidity put in place by the New Zealand Government, their recent actions seemed to be driven by short-term rather than wider social concerns.

The Parliamentary Select Committee wanted to know what we planned to do about these hidebound bank responses. Did we have the powers we needed? Given the fragility of the climate, we were reluctant to try and force the banks to do things that could have costly consequences, especially by threatening to use our deregistration powers. We had resolved to put more pressure on the bank chief executives, but this did not satisfy all the Committee members. The Opposition members announced their intention to carry out a public inquiry into the state of banking in New Zealand. They were keen for us to appear before them but, as they were not a full parliamentary committee, we declined the opportunity.

I discussed the attitudes of the banks with the Prime Minister and the Minister of Finance. They too wanted the banks to be more sensitive to New Zealand's commercial needs. I talked to each of the main bank chief executives on the phone over the next week. They seemed taken aback by the storm of criticism, vehemently arguing, and publicly, that offshore funding was still expensive. That was certainly true, though some of the New Zealand subsidiaries had so far made little effort to go offshore in search of long-term funding under the New Zealand Government guarantee. The chief executives also complained about how expensive it had become to get retail deposits. Traditionally these banks had funded themselves cheaply offshore and had not paid over-much attention to New Zealanders with funds to deposit. Now this was changing. We had long, sometimes difficult discussions.

A month or two later an olive branch was offered: could Toby Fiennes and I come to dinner with the four main bank chief executives to discuss matters? We dined in the presidential suite at Wellington's InterContinental Hotel. I have not the slightest recall of the food, but the conversation was interesting. The chief executives were now more reflective and accommodating. After being castigated daily by the media, they had seen their banks lose public standing and were looking to improve matters.

In the midst of this local battle, I had a respite offshore. Another meeting of central bank governors at the Bank for International Settlements in Basel was an opportunity to hear up-to-the-minute insights into the fight for recovery from the mouths of the front-line generals. It also gave me a brief chance to do something I had been putting off because of the crisis. My Board had been urging me to go to a chief executive leadership course and I very much wanted to do this. Now the opportunity arose for a couple of days at the INSEAD business school in Fontainebleau, en route to Basel, and I grabbed the chance. I was looking for reinvigoration, rejuvenation, modernisation. The Board thought I also needed rest and contemplation, but there would not be much time for these until the crisis abated.

I had to leave the course a day early to attend the Basel meeting. I got up at 3 a.m. (I had not been sleeping much anyway, because of jet-lag) and drove to Orly airport, south of Paris, to catch a dawn flight. The airport was nearly empty, its cafés closed. A few drowsy cleaners were sweeping up piles of litter. Sitting tired and dejected on a hard plastic bench, I reflected on the mess. Then I turned my attention to an unopened package given to me as I left INSEAD late the night before. It was a pile of surveyed opinions on my leadership from my colleagues in Wellington. Though some of the warm and inspiring tributes to my role at the Reserve Bank sounded worryingly like funeral eulogies, they gave me comfort and invigoration.

At the end of May the new government announced its first Budget. We had seen dire warnings from rating agencies and markets about the risks involved. Increasing government spending would have incurred a downgrade from one of the credit rating agencies, so the Minister had worked hard with Treasury to cut back low-quality spending. This was taken as a welcome signal by the markets.

Fiscal policy had worked reasonably well for New Zealand through this period, partly through good management and partly through luck. The Labour-led Government in the last two years of their term in office had increased spending on their programmes. In the crisis that had been helpful because it pushed funding into the economy and stimulated spending at a time when we needed it. The usual problem with using fiscal policy to apply a stimulus is that it can take a long time to put in place and too long to withdraw afterwards. Now we needed government spending to decrease as we pulled out of recession, so it would not add inflationary pressure. The Budget did not predict a return to growth until the 2010/11 year. In addition, the government sector took a huge hit. The budget surplus would be replaced by a deficit eventually to reach 5 per cent. Government gross debt was forecast to spiral from a very manageable 20 per cent of GDP to a figure over twice that.

On 28 May, immediately after the Budget, Standard & Poor's took us off the negative outlook (for our long-term foreign currency rating) and put us back on AA+ with stable outlook. We were pleased, especially since at that time Britain had been put on negative outlook for a downgrade, which caused a flurry around the markets, and Ireland was downgraded for a second time with a further negative outlook. But this relief was not to last long. Six weeks later Fitch Ratings, the third-biggest international credit rating agency, unexpectedly put the New Zealand Government long-term credit ratings on negative outlook. The pressure was still on.

The fifth of June is the birthday of both Adam Smith and John Maynard Keynes. It is also mine. My wife was on a working trip to the United Kingdom so I had a celebratory drink by myself, then went out to a New Zealand Symphony Orchestra concert at the Michael Fowler Centre. I sat next to a cabinet minister, who confided that we were to listen to a piece he had selected for his funeral. We had recently been discussing the concept of 'living wills' – being considered by Northern Hemisphere regulators in preparation for bank failures, but this admission caught me by surprise. It was a contemplative evening.

In a central bank, forecasting never stops. This time, as we prepared our June forecasts, there was a glimmer of relief in sight: for the first time for a year we could construct a picture of a more stable world. The financial markets showed some signs of recovery: the London Interbank Offered Rate (LIBOR, an important benchmark that banks use to charge each other for short-term lending) had at last fallen back below 1 per cent. Stock markets had been first to improve: they had recovered a third of their price declines and the mood was more buoyant. But no one could be sure of further recovery ahead. We were painfully aware that the Great Depression had seen a stock market recovery in 1932, only to fall away a year later and again in 1935.

The US banks had started to raise capital from the markets. On 10 June, amid much fanfare, ten of the largest US banks announced they would be able to repay the US Treasury monies lent nine months previously under the TARP bailout. A cynical public saw this as a way for the banks to avoid government-mandated restrictions on executive pay, but the news did reflect real improvement in the capital markets. And if May Day marked a bad time for the capitalist system, Goldman Sachs chose 14 July, Bastille Day, to announce that, through this quarter, they had actually earned a useful profit from trading activities, of which they would set aside $6.65 billion to pay bonuses.

The New Zealand financial markets had been considerably buoyed by the funding success of ANZ National Bank. It is the largest bank by a long way in New Zealand, and has been ever since it swallowed the operations of the National Bank, previously owned by Lloyds Bank. That gives it an important place in the markets. In March ANZ had secured the first offshore longer-term funding under the New Zealand Government guarantee. It was very expensive, paying about 7.5 per cent for three years, and set a high benchmark price for future issues. But in its own way, it was an important and trailblazing action.

Our traditional trading partners remained in dire straits. In late June the OECD predicted the thirty most industrialised nations would contract by 4 per cent during the year. There was a silver lining: they also prophesied the world economy nearing the bottom of its recession curve. For our part there was more good news: it looked like the Chinese Government's massive spending programme was bringing an abrupt return to growth for this resource-hungry economy. In turn, that provided cheerful news for a recovering Australian economy. In June the Australians announced that they had escaped recession altogether, the only OECD country to do so. (As a matter of statistical detail, had they measured their GDP using only a measure of production, as we do, they would have been marginally negative for two quarters – in recession.)

Could we see a New Zealand recovery? We had applied a lot of stimulus funds, but we needed market conditions that were conducive to recovery. We wanted low, stimulative interest rates but the combination of expensive markets and conservative banks aiming to protect their interest margins was not delivering them. This situation was back in the headlines when Opposition members of the Finance and Expenditure Committee produced their report on the banks, criticising them heavily.

We also wanted a competitive exchange rate to assist exporters to rebalance the New Zealand economy and to reduce the chances of an import-fuelled worsening of imbalance. But the international foreign exchange markets had other things in mind. They saw that economies like the United States were far more in need of rebalancing and in their assessment, seen from a distance, New Zealand (like Australia) was actually recovering rather well in comparison to the jaded Northern Hemisphere. In addition, as the markets gathered confidence they renewed their appetite for 'risk currencies', moving out of the US dollar. This pushed up commodity currencies, the New Zealand dollar among them.

At the Reserve Bank, as the New Zealand dollar rose we suffered a partial reversal of unrealised gains on our open FX position. In the month of May these paper losses were considerable, and caused some concern around the Bank. But our main worry was that the rising exchange rate did not provide New Zealand with the conditions for the long-term sustainable recovery that we would have liked.

Our June *Monetary Policy Statement* was the first to point to green shoots emerging. We tentatively speculated that June itself might mark the trough for the economy. We forecast a very weak recovery from there, though it probably would not feel like a real recovery because unemployment would rise further. We identified a likely pick-up in house prices and in other housing investment, but households had not yet managed to restructure their balance sheets. They were still very exposed to borrowing and cautious.

We decided not to reduce the OCR further at this stage but to leave it unchanged, at 2.5 per cent. However we took another gamble and

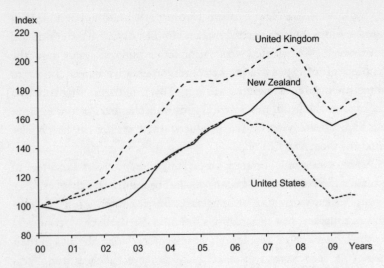

Index

The rise and fall of the housing markets: this graph measures the movements in real house prices during the boom and subsequent crisis. Source: Haver, RBNZ

repeated that we expected to keep rates down for at least a year. Our message to the banks was clear:

> We have cut the OCR by a large amount over the year. We expect the effects to pass through to more borrowers over coming quarters as existing fixed-rate mortgages come up for re-pricing. Although rising longer-term interest rates overseas are placing upward pressure on longer-term lending rates here, there is room for further reductions in shorter-term lending rates.
>
> The low OCR and stimulatory fiscal policy are the main sources of support to the New Zealand economy at present. It is likely to be some time before the recovery becomes self-sustaining and monetary policy support can be withdrawn.

CHAPTER 10

Fragile Recovery
June–August 2009

When the crisis struck and banks failed, commentators were swift to point the finger of blame. Financial journalists, analysts and academics expressed their views forcibly; arguments and counter-arguments criss-crossed the blogs. Bankers and stressed-out regulators also had firm opinions, but generally did not air them in public. Within central banks, internal debate raged back and forth. We urgently needed to understand the causes of these events so that we could counter them; but with bad news and uncertainty still swirling, it was too soon for mature reflection.

An early attempt to track the roots of the problems was made at a special conference run by the Bank for International Settlements in Basel in June 2009. A group of financial academics looked into what had gone wrong with the system. In the naive way of some academics, they were scathing: banks, boards, markets, regulations, politicians – all were to blame. I thought that some of this criticism was harsh, but then I was no detached onlooker. The commentators generally did not yet have good data to back their claims – that would take years to accumulate. But in the meantime drawing some conclusions was necessary, so we could work out what to do next.

There was a great deal of talk about the biggest banks, those categorised as 'too big to fail' because of their system-wide impacts. But was size the key factor, or did we really mean too *connected* to fail? Bear

155

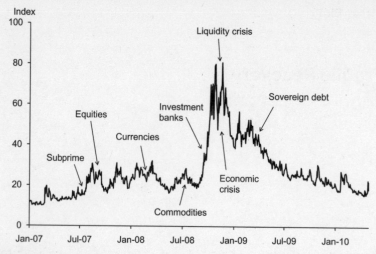

Index

Stages of the crisis: one market disruption led to another. The graph measures the Chicago Board Options Exchange Volatility Index (VIX), a measure of alarm in the financial market. Source: Bloomberg

Stearns had been deeply entwined with international counterparties. And what about the diverse global operations of Lehman Brothers – was the bank too *complex* to fail? Size, interrelatedness and complexity all played a role.

But how would we know what was too big, or connected, or complex? Once we had identified these institutions, something would have to be done. Should governments be explicit about the problem entities, acknowledge a governmental role, designate them, levy them in some way to pay for government backing? Could insurance handle the risk? Could large banks be bailed out? Could they actually be closed? Major banking problems had occurred in small countries such as Iceland, Ireland, Belgium, Switzerland. There the problem had seemed to be 'too big for the country'.

Many of the difficulties had arisen not in regulated banks but in investment banks and other institutions engaging in quasi-banking activities outside the purview of bank regulators. There was a general view that this would have to change, though there was no consensus about how. American investment banks in particular would try to game any new regulation intended to ring-fence them. (This point was underlined by Goldman Sachs' announcement on 14 July that it had grown its income well above predictions during the preceding three months, a period when it had been taking emergency TARP funds.) And some of the large banks seemed to have redesigned the rules of the game: stockholders providing capital took much cyclical risk, while executives enjoyed high returns through salaries and bonuses that seemed to have been de-risked.

Another governance worry related to the power and competence, or lack thereof, on the part of banks' chief risk officers and risk committees. These officers assess the possible outcomes from any deal and decide whether the risks are acceptable under the bank's mandated policies. We were now hearing about cases where risks had been miscalculated, procedures bypassed and officers overruled, all in the race for higher earnings.

The problems of risk assessment led to argument about the adequacy of international accounting standards. Did fair value accounting standards properly reflect earnings performance? Did 'mark-to-market' accounting requirements exacerbate financial problems when markets ceased to function properly? What about the incentives to over-distribute in good times and rely on government support in bad? One commentator noted that the re-capitalisation needed by three big American investment banks in the crisis approximately equalled the distributions made to their shareholders in the previous eight years.

There was even greater argument about what the fundamental problem with banks had been. Was it illiquidity (leading to an inability to fund immediate requirements) or basic insolvency (with liabilities exceeding assets)? Could regulators actually distinguish between the two?

In the 1960s and '70s, bank regulators had concentrated on ensuring banks had the liquid funds to meet likely calls. More recently the regulatory focus had moved to capital: the Basel I and Basel II regulatory systems laid down principles for how much capital a bank should have to support its operations. Through the crisis this had mainly worked: when conditions became more fragile the markets had demanded more and, when possible, banks had raised it. But liquidity had dried up in the crisis, even for well-capitalised banks in deep markets. It looked as though minimum liquidity requirements were necessary.

What about the role of the securitisation markets? The accepted view prior to the crisis had been that good securitisation would disperse credit risk to those best placed to bear it. In contrast, the development of structured subprime mortgage instruments seemed to have amplified risks as the chain of intermediaries lengthened.

If risks had increased, this brought into question the performance of the credit rating agencies who rated these packages, their incentives and their technical ability. From a mathematical viewpoint, institutions' modelling abilities had improved hugely, and the markets had come to rely on standard measures like value-at-risk (VAR). But even the best of these models had trouble incorporating extreme 'tail-end' financial risks under contingent events.

And if that was not enough, we were now learning about the limits of market efficiency when under stress – times when prices are unreliable, asset quality is impaired, information is uncertain, liquid securities become illiquid, buyers go on strike and markets fail to clear at any price.

Every question provoked another, and though every academic in the conference room had his or her pet theory, clear answers were rare. I could see these arguments still had a long way to go, for the facts were still changing around us. Based on these, the world's regulators were gearing up for a major re-think. This was occurring at Basel, home of the most important international bank regulatory body, the Basel Committee on Banking Supervision (BCBS). The Committee would feed its recommendations to the Financial Stability Board (FSB), which would take soundings from the other international standard-setters – the International Accounting Standards Board (IASB), the International Organization of Securities Commissions (IOSCO), the International Association of Insurance Supervisors (IAIS), the Committee on Payment and Settlement Systems (CPSS), the Global Stability Forum and others – a veritable network of regulatory bodies. The Financial Stability Board together with the IMF would then offer the combined views to the newly vigorous G-20, whose leaders planned to meet in Pittsburgh in October and had publicly committed to big changes.

If only it were so simple! Alongside these international efforts, the countries with large financial centres were already planning re-regulation, and here the heat of national politics was strong. Prime Minister Gordon Brown of the United Kingdom promised heavy taxes on free-riding bankers. President Sarkozy of France spoke of a stronger role for the French Government. In the United States the Financial Accounting Standards Board had already unilaterally changed accounting standard policies; there was intense debate in the US Congress about how to supervise US banks; and no assurance that international efforts would be approved in the States.

There were further moves afoot in the regions. The European Central Bank had been monitoring financial stability for most but not all EU member countries; the European Commission had controls over some banking practices; national finance ministers and central banks had further powers; and, in many but not all countries, specialist banking supervisors had primary responsibility. To that complicated network was added a new body, the European Systemic Risk Board, with a complex governance structure reflecting all these interests.

In New Zealand monetary policy, bank supervision and financial stability roles are filled by the Reserve Bank (and by the Minister of Finance and Treasury where public funds are involved). We have a much simpler regulatory system (and a much simpler banking system). Some of the proposed international institutions and processes looked extremely clumsy to us. Furthermore, they could propose changes – which could affect us – that we might think unnecessary, but as we have no representation on most of these bodies we also have no direct way to influence them.

When it came to finger-pointing, we in New Zealand got off relatively easily. While we'd had our share of healthy argument between government and regulators, disagreements had not been fundamental. But in Basel I heard of growing tensions in other countries between central banks, treasuries and ministers. In Europe German Chancellor Angela Merkel had criticised Anglo-American quantitative easing, there was trouble among the European Central Bank countries and several ECB governors were publicly criticised by their own ministers;

in the central and southern Americas, some governors became politically involved. The Mexican governor was not re-appointed and the Argentinean governor was unceremoniously ejected from the Bank. In Britain there were reported political differences with the Bank of England. And, in the United States, Chairman Bernanke at times faced a hostile Congress.

Over the preceding few years, the Bank for International Settlements had provided a rare voice among international agencies, warning of the catastrophic risk of bank failures. Its then chief economist, Bill White, had not always convinced the sceptics, but his warnings had been clear. At the bank's annual meeting in Basel, new general manager Jaime Caruana, a softly spoken Spaniard, now presented his view of the world economy. He saw financial markets at last looking towards recovery. He thought the older industrialised centres of the world were still in very bad shape, but emerging market economies and commodity exporters (Australia, New Zealand, South Africa, Brazil, Chile, Argentina, Indonesia) looked more solid. It was a two-tier world. Caruana said that, despite continuing fragility and weaknesses, it was time for countries to prepare an exit from government stimulus policies and plan the recovery.

Caruana also listed some of the things that could go wrong: financial strife not dealt with, the economic recovery too fragile, renewed financial market volatility, potential growth tracking lower than before the crisis, imbalanced economies not rebalancing, trade protection growing, the private sector drivers of growth not emerging and so on. The pitfalls seemed endless. Finally, Caruana admitted that the old norms had gone forever, and we did not yet know what the 'new normal' would look like.

The BIS annual report presented at these meetings is always a treasure trove of data. This time we got a graphic picture of the ballooning volume of derivatives in the lead-up to the bubble bursting. One graph showed the growth of trade in credit default swap derivatives (a gross number admittedly somewhat theoretical, because they would never all be on the market at once). As economists we are accustomed to talking in billions of dollars. During the crisis we had had to measure rescue packages in trillions. But the graph showed that gross derivatives growth had scaled new heights. In 2007 it had reached almost a quadrillion dollars!

I arrived back in Wellington in late June, with the end of our financial year now close. It is a critical time for us – we have a large balance sheet to check, accounts to put together, auditing to do, reports for the Board. The Reserve Bank is funded by seigniorage: we issue notes and coins to the public. A bank note costs much less to print than the amount at which we sell it to the banks – $5, $10, $20 or whatever. (Coinage is not quite such a money-spinner, because the coins are worth less.) This seigniorage earns us about $200 million per year for the taxpayer. We have a five-year funding agreement with government that allows us to use about $40 to $50 million of the Bank's revenue each year to run the Bank. In addition, the government has over the years contributed capital of about $1.6 billion to stand behind the risks inherent in our business. Quite reasonably, the government wants to see a return on its capital. Depending on our trading results over the year, the Bank pays this as an annual dividend.

Our balance sheet also shows our holdings of funds to back the $4 billion claims of the public on our currency; these are invested to earn a return. We hold another, larger amount to run the Crown Settlement Account and to handle overnight liquidity in the banking markets. And we hold significant foreign reserves for crisis or cyclical intervention in the financial market. These funds and amounts may sound somewhat arcane, but they are huge sums of money and good or poor management makes a massive difference. A central bank *can* lose money, but this should never be for reasons of bad management, and we are very cautious. Furthermore, the eyes of the auditor-general and the financial press are always on central bank balance sheets, and when you are also a bank regulator, you need to model best practice for the banks as well.

The 2008/09 year was very unusual in terms of balance sheet management. In 2007 our balance sheet had totalled around NZ$22 billion, and now it had grown to $36 billion. There were several reasons. We had changed the way we manage domestic banking settlement to a 'cashed-up' payments system, leaving the banks with much larger cash balances that were remunerated at the OCR rather than fine-tuned on a day-to-day basis. This change added approximately $8 billion to our balance sheet.

As we accepted a much wider range of securities (those residential mortgage-backed securities, for example) in return for providing liquidity to the banks, we also increased the risk on our balance sheet. Most of this security was still very good quality and had remained so through the crisis, but it nevertheless presented more challenges than government credit.

Our foreign reserves position was more complicated. We had increased our foreign reserve assets and built up an open FX position, having bought foreign currency during the period from mid-2007 to mid-2008 when the dollar was strong, then sold some of it as the currency weakened through 2008–2009. Thus things were positive: the New Zealand-dollar value of our foreign currency assets and liabilities rose as the local exchange rate depreciated, and our open position had increased in value hugely. However, not all this value had been realised (in other words, the trading positions had not all been closed and cashed up). The final equation would depend on a complex mix of exchange rates and interest rates, but overnight movements in the US–NZ dollar exchange rate had major effects. I anxiously checked the rate each morning, because it could affect our results by many millions of dollars.

We had not entered these open foreign exchange positions with the aim of making money, however. Unlike most currency traders, we were making long-term decisions for policy reasons. In addition, we knew that in some years the currency would go against us. But in this *annus horribilis* it was certainly nice to be making a good profit, knowing that out there in the financial markets there was a group of currency traders who had been betting on a non-competitive currency and had paid the price.

The flipside was that these much bigger financial assets had to be continually managed, and this itself was tough. The rapidly changing investment credit situation meant risks had increased. Our risk unit sets parameters to keep the quality of our investments high – we limit our traders to dealing in highly rated vanilla securities. But as the bad news had spread, many corporate entities were rapidly downgraded. We had a tough job liquidating positions in newly risky investments. Our traders also found they were very limited in what they could trade, as the triple-A sector shrank and other investors also looked for quality. Trading returns sank.

But so far we had lost nothing to credit failures around the world, a great relief. We had also benefited from preparation: our efficient new electronic treasury system allowed us to keep track of the increase in complex trades; our membership of the CLS system let us settle international foreign exchange deals with reduced time-of-day risk; and the renegotiation of International Swaps and Derivatives Association (ISDA) agreements that govern trades allowed us to reduce credit risk in FX swap deals. We were also lucky: because New Zealand banks had not taken the same risks as their overseas counterparts, we had not had to trigger major 'lender-of-last-resort' exercises with banks.

By year end, when we subtracted costs, the Reserve Bank had made a net profit on all its operations of over $900 million. We paid the government a dividend of $630 million, a useful contribution in a year when some of its revenue sources were drying up. The balance sheet expansion was happening to other central banks, too, as they looked to inject extra liquidity into the financial system. The biggest balance sheet of all belonged to the US Federal Reserve System. Their total assets grew from about $800 billion pre-crisis to $2.2 trillion during the crisis as, first, direct injections to the banks and then mortgage-backed security purchases were undertaken. Some of these measures mean normality will take longer to return.

We had earlier asked the banks for information – weekly data on how they were funding themselves and how long their current funding would last – to help us monitor them. The average maturity of funding on their books had fallen through late 2008, and we had been urging the banks to seek longer-term funding, even if they had to pay a lot. In principle they had agreed that that was sensible, but in practice it was not proving easy to obtain. But now, at last, as we scanned the weekly numbers I could see some early signs of lengthening maturities. In many cases, the banks' treasurers had packed their bags and were off travelling around New York, Tokyo, London and some of the continental European markets looking for funds, using the New Zealand Government's Wholesale Guarantee Scheme. They were reporting some early successes in raising money, albeit small amounts at expensive prices. They were having to pay margins of more than 200 basis points over US Treasury bond yields, which was going to hold up average funding costs for some time. It was not business as usual, but it was a distinct improvement.

At the same time the banks had rediscovered retail deposits. Smaller savers, often older people, were abandoning finance company debentures and returning to what they saw as safe havens, traditional bank savings accounts. And with offshore funding difficult, the banks were prepared to pay more for these deposits.

A major reason for shoring up funding was pressure from rating agencies who, keen to recover reputation and focusing on risks, were pressuring Australian banks to hold longer-term funds. Another driver was our new liquidity policy. We had been researching this prior to the crisis and, while new international measures to improve liquidity were also under way, these could take years to put in place. We decided to move ahead with two key requirements: each bank had to meet a 'mismatch ratio', to ensure that they could cover likely demands for funds in a crisis situation, over a week and over a month. In addition, they were required to meet a core funding ratio, so that their share of 'sticky' funds (which we define as customer funding plus market funding for longer than a year) would stay above a certain percentage. We mentioned a possible percentage to the banks, and they objected: meeting it would be overly expensive. After doing some calibration work we agreed with them, and initially settled the ratio at 65 per cent, gradually to rise to 75 per cent.

The banks were still in the political spotlight – under fire for not fully passing on the OCR cuts. We had promised the Parliamentary Select Committee to investigate banks' interest rate margins further, and on 6 July we published our report. It was carefully written, trying to clarify a complex financial picture, without vilifying the banks or entering a highly politicised debate. We concluded that, while a large part of the OCR cuts had been passed on to borrowers, about 100 to 150 basis points had been offset by higher marginal funding costs.

As the financial markets improved, the banks reassessed their funding and in both Australia and New Zealand they started to expand longer-term borrowings. They continued to fret about expensive foreign capital markets, and they resented having to pass on a similar premium to local depositors. Bad debts also started to emerge on their lending books. Most of these concerned small businesses or farms where borrowers had over-committed themselves at a time of high property and farm prices. There were also residential mortgage defaults followed by evictions and mortgagee sales, but these were mercifully rare. Foreclosures attracted considerable media and political criticism.

In the case of some of the agricultural defaults, we felt that certain banks had been over-optimistic and under-analytical in their lending, and we moved to tighten the relevant capital requirements for the future. The banks complained bitterly. But generally they seemed to have learned from the early '90s downturn in New Zealand and, this time, their overall risk management was better. Late repayments and other signs of distress were being monitored and managed carefully. The banks might have preferred to make bigger provisions for likely future losses, but ironically the international accounting standards had limited the amount to which they could do this. Although non-performing assets were mounting through this period, it looked like they might peak at around 2 per cent of assets, far less than in some earlier downturns and manageable for banks and the economy.

By this time the troubles in financial markets meant that there were only fourteen banks in the world still rated AA and above – including all four of the Australians. This was very important for our financial system and made crisis management easier. Perhaps understandably, it also meant the banks were coming across as rather arrogant at a time when other firms were struggling. The Australian banks also indicated to us that they considered the New Zealand market rather boring as they surveyed new opportunities in East Asia, mid-America and the north of Britain. After the stress of the previous year, 'boring' seemed just fine to us.

Gradually we felt comfortable enough to reduce our extra scrutiny of the bank balance sheets. The non-bank sector was another story. Many finance companies and building societies had joined the government's Retail Deposit Guarantee Scheme, offering them temporary protection. As the scheme was to terminate in October 2010, many finance companies had been offering debentures that were due to expire at that time. This was starting to distort the term structure of funding. The building societies and credit unions still mainly looked healthy, with simple balance sheets and loyal members. Some smaller finance companies looked fragile, but could probably be managed into quiet termination.

Depositors' money was safe, guaranteed by government. But taxpayers were still exposed to the possibility of some finance companies failing within the scheme. In the Budget, Treasury assessed the potential losses associated with the guarantee scheme at between $650 million and $700 million.

We focused more on the medium-sized finance companies. Our analysts had done some sound work looking at balance sheets, business plans and prospects. There were a lot of bad loans to be worked through and balance sheets to be recapitalised. I was more interested in what phoenixes might arise from the ashes. New Zealand would need reliable medium-sized financial institutions in the future. And credibility would ultimately depend on access to funding and balance sheet stability.

Around this time we had visits from a number of local financial institutions, wanting to discuss matters. Some of them were talking about possible mergers. From our own point of view this could be desirable. We had been studying it ourselves, but the restructurings would have to be done from within the industry. Certainly their poor loan books would have to be cleaned up first. It was somewhat frustrating seeing what had to be done, but knowing that we were not the right people to do it.

In our new role as supervisor of non-bank institutions, we were still working to apply the higher standards for non-bank deposit-takers. In the meantime, however, we needed to address what would happen when the retail guarantee terminated. With so much ongoing uncertainty, we advised that the scheme should be extended for another year, but with tougher entry conditions and higher fees to reduce the scope for finance companies to game it.

In late July I was off again on a brief trip to Hong Kong. The Hong Kong Monetary Authority (HKMA) was hosting a meeting of East Asian and Pacific governors to review the crisis. The meeting was held in the rocket-shaped skyscraper that houses the HKMA, the tallest building on Hong Kong Island. The top floors command a huge panorama towards the hills of mainland China, but usually these are shrouded in smog. Now for the first time I could see them clearly, marking out the New Territories. So many Chinese factories in the Pearl River Delta had closed during the crisis that the air had had a chance to clear, the first time for many decades.

These meetings are quiet, closed-door affairs. I found my colleagues in much better moods than when we had last met. Things were improving. Industrial production had picked up markedly, an important precursor to growth in the manufacturing powerhouse of East Asia. Some governors were irritated with the United States for not managing its financial institutions better. They still bore the scars from the East Asian crisis a decade earlier; the tough prescriptions of the IMF rescue operations at that time still grated with some governors.

The East Asian recovery, however, was well ahead of that of the Northern economies and the governors were optimistic. At the same time they realised that their growth strategies of lower exchange rates, high savings and export-led growth driven by Western consumers might ultimately be unsustainable.

The news from China was particularly heartening. We find it difficult to understand that massive economy. The huge government spending programme from six months earlier seemed to be working as intended – there was big infrastructure expenditure particularly in remote inland provinces. Their construction needs were fuelling strong growth in iron ore, coal and other industrial imports. Much of this was coming from Australia – its China-share of exports had doubled from 13 per cent to 26 per cent in just a year. The story for New Zealand was more muted, but Chinese demand for dairy and forestry meant our China export share had nearly doubled too, from about 5 per cent to 10 per cent. It would not be long before China would be our second biggest export market after Australia, replacing the United States, but this new relationship would need very careful handling.

We were now in the later stages of the crisis. Governments had been

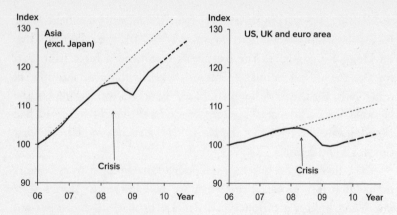

A tale of two recoveries: the graphs show strong GDP recovery in Asia and weak recovery in the West. Source: Haver, RBNZ

rescuing private financial ventures left, right and centre. Now there was a bill to be paid. At the meeting we discussed the proposition that long-term real interest rates in the major economies were set to rise as a result of these big increases in public debt. The research estimated that every 1 per cent increase in the debt to GDP ratio would raise the long-term government bond yield by 5 basis points. Given the mounting official debt, this looked enough to have a substantial effect on world interest rates into the future, possibly crowding out private investment and reducing potential growth rates. It could also be big enough to make it difficult to calculate appropriate monetary policy settings for the future.

I returned to New Zealand feeling more strongly than ever that, given our reliance on foreign capital, mounting foreign interest rates could cause us problems.

I soon got a chance to bring this matter up. A few days after my return, my assistant, Sandy Anderson, was surprised to answer the phone and find it was the Prime Minister on the line. Could he pop over and have a chat with Alan about the economy? We had a quick visit from a security officer checking out the venue (no problem – central banks tend to be very secure because of their cash-handling requirements). And then John Key himself arrived, casual, relaxed and just wanting to test some views and talk about productivity and competitiveness, all in the context of improving New Zealand's place in the OECD. We had an agreeable discussion for an hour, interrupted only by increasingly pointed phone messages from his office reminding him of all the other things he had to do. He left reluctantly.

In the midst of all these happenings we had another event to deal with, something to celebrate. On 1 August 1934, the doors of the Reserve Bank of New Zealand had opened for business. Following the turbulence of the 1920s, the New Zealand Government became concerned about managing its own exchange rate, its ability to raise funds in offshore markets and its foreign reserves. The Bank of England allowed Otto Niemeyer, a senior officer on a trip to Australia, South Africa and Canada, to visit New Zealand and he advised on how to set up a central bank. The process took some years and it was 1934 before an act of Parliament established the Bank. By this time New Zealand was in severe depression.

Because we were in recession we did not think it would be appropriate to spend a lot of money on a ritzy celebration, but we wanted to mark our 75th anniversary somehow. We started the week by giving each staff member a tiny 75th anniversary cake. We opened an exhibition on the Bank's history in our museum. We had a period dress-up day, where each department wore the clothes of a different decade. And on Saturday night we had a 1930s-themed dinner dance with everyone clad in appropriate fashion, dancing the Charleston.

We had invited a special guest to give a lecture to mark the anniversary. This was Sir Howard Davies who had run the British bank regulator, the Financial Services Authority, and was now director of the London School of Economics. Howard told us the story of a conversation he'd had with Queen Elizabeth II, when she had recently visited the LSE. 'Why did nobody see the crisis coming?' the queen had asked. Sir Howard argued that it was too early to apportion blame, but that bankers, regulators, economists, central banks and borrowers might all be criticised. He concluded with a cartoon of a group of British economists congratulating themselves on having answered the queen's questions at a visit to Buckingham Palace. Out of their sight, in the background, we see the queen summoning her public executioner to sharpen his axe.

At the end of August it was back to the rolling plains and soaring mountains of Wyoming for the US Federal Reserve conference at Jackson Hole. There we gathered again in the lodge with its panoramic views of the Grand Teton Range, in the same room where I had listened in 2005 to early warning signs of world recession. The mood was sombre as top academics, bankers and central bank governors discussed the state of the world. I chaired one of the day's proceedings, a difficult job when there were so many personalities in the room determined to contribute.

By now the crisis had been going long enough for researchers to gather data and make comparisons. A study by economists Carmen Reinhart and Ken Rogoff of eight centuries of financial crises shows that when an economic crisis also involves a banking crisis it can be particularly severe. A banking crisis might typically last for two years or so, followed by a weak recovery. Now other researchers added to the conditions: a crisis would be particularly severe if there were sudden, unforeseeable surprises such as market-stops, if risk were excessively concentrated in systemic financial institutions and if early policy responses were slow. Unfortunately many of those conditions had been seen in the global financial crisis.

Economists have come a long way in explaining and predicting how economies behave. Macro-economic models give fairly good predictions. Unfortunately the same is not yet true for financial models. We heard about research attempts to model financial crises. We can now measure a country's vulnerability to crisis but not the length of time or depth to which it might be exposed. Financial variables such as credit growth and interest rates do provide some indications, but their overall explanatory power is poor. And macro-economic factors that we would instinctively think of as important, such as domestic savings rates, do not seem to affect the modelling. Overall, the models of financial distress still looked unsophisticated and of limited use to central bankers.

The speakers were more upbeat on how governments had reacted to the crisis. Some academics thought we central banks had been slow off the mark – but hindsight is a wonderful thing. Traditional monetary policy, non-traditional credit easing and lending guarantees appeared to have had real impacts. The century-old guiding dictum of Walter Bagehot, founding editor of *The Economist*, was that central banks should lend liberally on good security to illiquid banks through their lender-of-last resort facility, and this had occurred during the global crisis. But speakers pointed out the practical problems of distinguishing between illiquid and insolvent companies, between systemic and non-systemic operations, and between traditional banks and all the other users of liquidity: primary dealers, investment banks and money funds.

Using monetary policy is not the only way to help stabilise an economy. There had been a consensus view that automatic fiscal stabilisers (less tax taken in a recession, and more paid out on unemployment benefits and other assistance) make a useful contribution to stabilisation too. Generally economists have felt that due to practical problems like timing lags, small multipliers, perverse expectations and exit problems, discretionary fiscal policy is not a good stabilisation tool. But new research suggested that for a long and deep crisis like this one, fiscal stimulus was proving useful. The effects looked lower for tax cuts and higher for anything suggesting permanent increases in government consumption, as well as for psychologically attractive programmes (such as the US auto industry subsidy called 'cash for clunkers').

Discussion was not limited to monetary and fiscal policy solutions. Could we run policies targeting financial stability? Tradable insurance credits were suggested. The United States was considering a 'corridor system' of cash management, very similar to our own approach in New Zealand. We heard about compulsory discount windows, lender-of-last-resort tools for market systems, 'too big to fail' taxes and requirements to hold more capital. Academics were quick to offer their own solutions.

We spent the afternoons at Jackson Hole hiking. In the shade of a birch forest, we might walk around a reflecting lake, enjoying the scenery and discussing the wildlife (moose, beavers and bears). But the crisis was never far from our conversation.

I had been aware as I sat on the platform and surveyed the room that afternoon that some familiar faces were missing. Some were victims of the crisis, like the governor of the Bank of Iceland. Others could not attend because the economic or political situations in their home countries were too fraught. Some weary-looking colleagues had visibly aged. I knew personally of several who were fighting cancers.

At dinner I sat with several other central bankers, among them Ben Bernanke. He was quiet and reserved, as usual, but he deserved to nurse a quiet sense of satisfaction that the untested policies he had been forced to put in place seemed to be bearing fruit. Bernanke was facing considerable criticism in the media and in Congress, and rumours about his replacement had been rife in the gossipy world of financial markets. When he was re-nominated for Federal Reserve chairman by President Obama the following day, there was a palpable sense of relief among his fellow governors.

The two other central bank governors at the dinner table with me were quite dissimilar, though they had both been through trying times. Tito Mboweni, governor of the Reserve Bank of South Africa, was an ex-ANC guerrilla who was now fighting a very different battle, and doing it well. The other guest was Sinan al-Shabibi, governor of the Central Bank of Iraq. His problems made ours seem very minor: how to protect his staff, get currency safely to Iraqis around the country and help to rebuild a war-torn country. Both Tito and Sinan were positive about what lay ahead. That was an inspiration.

The folksy atmosphere of Jackson Hole remained charmingly untouched by world events. One of the world's top central bankers recounted that he had asked for a copy of the *Wall Street Journal* in the lodge's general store. 'Do you want yesterday's or today's?' asked the storekeeper. 'Today's, of course,' replied the central banker. 'Well then,' said the man, 'you had best come back tomorrow.' The story resonated. It would not be until tomorrow that we would truly be able to understand what was happening today.

CHAPTER 11

Bring Out Your Dead

Istanbul traffic is clogged, chaotic and noisy at the best of times. In early October 2009 it was worse than ever. Belching diesel trucks, yellow *taksis* and large tourist buses all competed for road space with convoys of official cars and squads of *polis*. Around Taksim Square, a detachment of soldiers complete with armed cars and water cannon was on duty. The occasion was the annual meetings of the IMF and the World Bank, a circus with up to 30,000 world leaders, staffers, politicians, bureaucrats and bankers in attendance.

To ensure the personal security of our low-key New Zealand delegation, we had been assigned a protection squad – a group of sullen, gun-toting young men with no English and even less humour. They trailed us everywhere (which somehow did not increase my sense of safety), even escorting us to our bedrooms at night. However, after dark we managed to lose them, sneaking out the side door of the hotel to hang out in a local dive for baklava and Turkish coffee.

Once at the conference, IMF economic counsellor and ex-MIT professor Olivier Blanchard gave us his view of the global recovery. After two dismal quarters of contraction, world growth had at last become slightly positive in the second quarter, and this was expected to strengthen. A normal cyclical recovery would see businesses regroup, expand production and build up stock, followed quickly by customers resuming their buying. But this recovery looked like it might be different, starting from a very low uncertain base, and with the stimulus coming from treasuries and central banks rather than the private sector.

Moving from fragile recovery to robust growth, Blanchard continued, would require several things. First, private sector demand in the form of household consumption and business investment would need to reawaken. But world output had dropped so far that there remained huge amounts of unused capacity, whether in coastal Chinese factories or in American banks.

Secondly, because government debt had risen hugely, government spending would need to be cut. The public sector debt of the G-20 countries had risen to 120 per cent of GDP and was forecast to worsen, not improve. In the meantime, people were likely to want to build up savings and that would not help the world's economy recover.

Thirdly, Blanchard argued, world demand needed to be rebalanced. Asia and particularly China needed to rebuild domestic consumption. Normally this might be expected to occur through interest rate adjustments and Asian exchange rates rising, but these did not look likely. Americans had to learn to save and Chinese had to learn to spend – though no one was optimistic about this happening soon.

Blanchard's three points were clear. But how to go about finding solutions to the problems he listed? From the vantage point of May 2010, the opportunities look mixed. Growth in East and South Asia has largely recovered, though this time driven more by regional than trans-Pacific demand. The Asian countries have surpassed their previous GDP peaks and look likely to fully recover 'lost' output. Stimulus policies have driven infrastructure investment in China and elsewhere, and this has led to strong demand for industrial materials around the world. Australia in particular has enjoyed booming exports of iron ore, coal, gas and other minerals to China and a massive terms-of-trade boost. Other major exporters of raw materials such as Brazil, Canada, Chile and South Africa have also done well. And stimulated by demand from Asia, New Zealand, Argentina, Indonesia and other exporters of soft commodities and food have benefited from rising prices

In the older Western countries the recovery has been slower and less certain. Hurt by falling house prices and fears of unemployment,

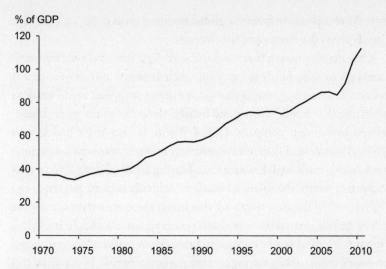

% of GDP

Western government debt grows alarmingly: the graph measures purchasing-power-parity-weighted gross public debt in G-7 countries as a percentage of GDP. Government debt was similarly high after World War II, but has not been as high in recent years. Source: IMF

households have lacked the confidence to spend, being more intent on paying back debt and building up savings. Faced with businesses operating on low turnover, the last thing managers have had on their minds is expansion through investment and recruitment.

With unsteady growth marked by continuing high unemployment and company failures, governments have been slow to remove stimulus measures and cut spending. This has further pushed up extremely high levels of government debt. In the OECD, net government borrowing as a percentage of world savings is estimated to have risen in the crisis from 5 per cent to almost 30 per cent. More worryingly, the IMF estimates that the gross public debt of the G-7 countries is now well above 100 per cent of GDP, its highest level since the days of the reconstruction after World War II.

How likely is a further slump, the so-called 'double-dip' scenario? As research by Carmen Reinhart and Ken Rogoff suggests, a financial crisis combined with an economic crisis – as we have just experienced – leads to a much slower recovery than either event would have produced on its own. As recuperation from the global financial crisis continues, we have already seen false dawns and new worries.

One major concern is around the sovereign markets, where governments go to raise funds to carry out their business and to finance any deficits. In late 2009, the Dubai Government surprised world markets by stating that it might not stand behind the debts of the government-related investment company Dubai World. If ever there had been a physical manifestation of over-investment in ostentatious infrastructure, it was in this small Arab Emirate state. Having financed these investments without concern, the financial markets suddenly became negative. The Dubai credit default swap spread, that market instrument measuring the risk of default, soared from 310 basis points to around 660. In itself, this Dubai risk would not be enough to bring down markets, but it directed investors' focus to the growing areas of government risk. In one sense this is not surprising. For several years, governments around the world have been rescuing poor private performers and bringing some of their risks on to government balance sheets. Even as governments assumed the risk, tax revenues had been falling and demand for social spending rising. A government has more financial credibility than a corporate because of its ability to tax, but this credibility is not unlimited. In 2009 and 2010, as financial markets realised the extent of the risk that governments had taken on, they reacted harshly.

From Dubai, the markets turned their gaze on Eastern Europe, where stressed countries such as Latvia and the Ukraine were made to cut spending deeply as a condition of IMF rescue programmes. Next in the spotlight were the PIIGS. The repercussions for these countries were different: as they all use the euro, there was no scope for individual currency depreciation. Ireland took tough action, cutting wages, salaries and benefits. The markets approved and Ireland's credit default swap spreads reduced from a high of almost 460 basis points to less than 200, though this still represented a big penalty on borrowing.

Greece was up next. The markets identified it as having poor statistics and poor fiscal management, and Greece's credit default swap spreads leapt over 800 basis points in May 2010. The Europeans, in their desperate search for a solution to stem the contagion before

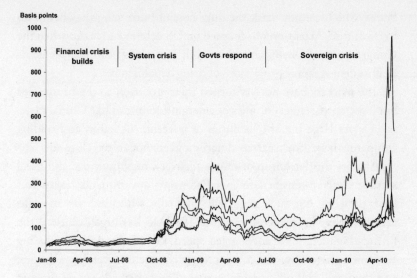

Basis points

| Financial crisis builds | System crisis | Govts respond | Sovereign crisis |

Sovereign risks take the crisis to a new stage: the graph shows the sovereign credit default swap spreads – a measure of the risk of governments defaulting on their debt – for Portugal, Ireland, Italy, Greece and Spain (the PIIGS). The highest line is for Greece. Source: Bloomberg and RBNZ calculations

it spread, agreed to a large joint IMF–European-Union-funded financial assistance package for Greece. The difficulties in negotiating this package reflect the difficulty that the European Monetary System has in exacting fiscal discipline when there is no individual exchange rate to assist and no regional fiscal authority. The events in Greece provoked fears that sovereign risk contagion could spread to other small economies that have government funding pressures or high debt levels. To head off this fate, affected governments have little alternative to swingeing budget cuts, even though these will slow their recovery.

The G-3 economies are also now coming under closer scrutiny. The markets are still digesting the implications of the current conditions in Japan, where official debt is at nearly 200 per cent of GDP and the population is declining; the United Kingdom, which has a new coalition government and where the Bank of England has been holding a significant share of outstanding government bonds; and the United

States, which cannot mask the huge cost of borrowing they bequeath to the future. Attention was focused on US debt in early 2010 when the Congress passed Obama's healthcare bill, increasing health entitlements against demographic projections of rising dependency.

The markets have not yet turned their attention to the prosperous but less transparent economies of emerging countries like China. Here, savings are large but the liabilities of government banks and trading companies have grown extraordinarily and are not always clear-cut.

Against this backdrop of fragile recovery, ongoing risks, and fiscal sectors under intensified financial scrutiny, governments themselves have to work out how they will gradually withdraw the stimulus measures they have been providing. The IMF has urged caution; the financial markets have encouraged speed. Generally speaking, the big economies have now pulled back their emergency liquidity schemes, and these will roll off as debts mature. Governments have terminated many special industry assistance schemes, but high unemployment means increased social spending continues. Bank wholesale funding guarantees are being terminated, though retail guarantees remain.

The next important step is the removal of monetary stimulus by raising policy interest rates from their historical lows back towards a more typical level. Australia, with its strong economy, has led the way on removing monetary stimulus. The challenge for the big economies is to pick the right time and speed to raise interest rates, and to learn the lesson of the East Asian crisis, when some central banks held on too low, for too long. But the current levels of international stimulation are unprecedented, and removing this stimulus – at very different rates across countries – will not be easy.

By the start of 2010 a recovery in New Zealand was in sight. The Reserve Bank's forecasts had pointed to a return to growth in the third quarter of 2009, and these proved to be correct. When we got the official GDP figures for the last quarter of 2009, we at the Bank breathed a collective sigh of relief: the constantly fluctuating data and nasty surprises of the previous year had lessened, and we felt confident in our forecasts again.

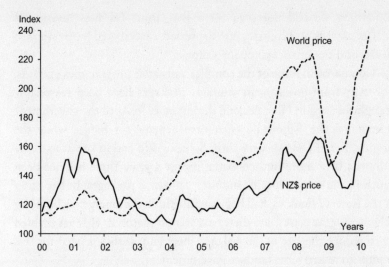

Export commodity prices drive the recovery: this graph shows the commodity price index for New Zealand exports in world prices and adjusted for the New Zealand exchange rate. Source: ANZ

The figures showed that we were on track towards a more robust recovery. There was growth of almost 1 per cent for the quarter, an improvement driven by stronger East Asian and Australian growth and good commodity prices for exports. Despite the stubborn strength of the New Zealand dollar, our balance of payments at last showed improvement, the external deficit reducing quite spectacularly from 9 per cent to 2 per cent (although, as ever in economics, such good news tends to be temporary).

Initially we feared that New Zealanders, judging the recession to be over, might start reinvesting in high-priced housing. Indeed, house prices, which had not dropped much, started to recover. But perhaps I underestimated New Zealanders' financial caution: no housing boom has so far followed. Instead, householders have been paying off mortgages and credit cards to reduce debt, consumption has stayed low, and there seems to be relatively little interest in house sales and new house building. Mortgage lending to householders has slowed considerably. In the business sector, bank credit actually reduced, something we had not seen for a long time. Business investment remained weak and construction depressed, exacerbated by the stress in the second-tier finance company sector.

Compared to some of the complex assistance programmes overseas, our exits from government stimulus packages have been reasonably straightforward in New Zealand during 2010. In April the government terminated the Wholesale Guarantee Scheme for banks, while the original Retail Deposit Guarantee Scheme is to end in late 2010, to be followed by a more limited extension for a year. There has not been much in the way of specific industry assistance packages. In late 2009 at the Reserve Bank we had begun paring back the emergency liquidity schemes for the banks, and these have all now matured. That has enabled us to reduce the size of our balance sheet and, with less need for risk capital, to return some funds to government.

That accomplished, the way is clear for monetary policy to orchestrate a gradual return to more normal conditions. Monetary policy is designed to exert incremental pressures on the economy in a controlled way. The challenge for New Zealand now (as in many other countries) is that things have changed: deposits and term market funding cost more, bank interest margins have increased, businesses and households are more cautious and household mortgages are of shorter duration.

It is a new world and none of us can be quite sure what concepts like 'normal' or 'neutral' now mean, nor how long it will be until interest rates are back at these levels. But we will surely find our way to some sort of equilibrium in the years ahead.

Both laypersons and specialists watched the financial sector become more and more sophisticated over the past decade – and were then surprised at how vulnerable it proved to be when things went wrong. As the financial crisis eased in the first half of 2010, I had a chance to reflect on the lessons we could take from the shocks of the last couple of years. A few key points struck me:

- The modern international global system has made great strides in its efficient provision of financial services, but its risk management has been less adept.

- There have been serious weaknesses in product design, markets, institutional arrangements, governance and regulation, with serious miscalculation of correlated tail-end risks contingent on other risks.
- Global banks can cause major disruption across financial systems; they need strong global regulators. Even small banks can cause major disruptions if they have global connections and are under-regulated.
- Shortage of liquidity can bring down a bank; liquidity and solvency are not as separate, as we had thought.
- Quarterly profit targets can be a dangerous driver of short-term financial decisions.
- It is difficult to define core banking and hard to confine banks to it.
- The international 'plumbing' – payments, settlement and clearance systems – worked well, but can't themselves block contagion.
- The financial sector is particularly difficult to regulate, because banks have scope to find creative ways around barriers and cause others to pay for their risk-taking.
- The relationship between banks and governments has fundamentally changed as a result of 'too big to fail', bailouts and their effects on moral hazard.

In the wake of the financial crisis, politicians and international regulators started asking fundamental questions. What do banks actually do? How does that contribute to society? And how much might our banking system be costing us? The political drive for reform has led to proposals for regulating executive remuneration, altering management incentives, taxing super-profits, levying systemically important banks and compulsorily divesting core commercial banking from other activities.

Through the Financial Stability Board, international regulators have proposed a number of ways to reduce the risk of bank failure in the future: a leverage ratio to prevent over-lending; a tightening of capital adequacy conditions to counter over-creative capital instruments; and liquidity ratios to weather a sudden dry-up of funding. In addition, regulators hoping to make bank failures less costly have suggested requirements for 'contingent capital', to improve robustness under stress, and 'living wills', to clarify resolution on closure. The accounting standards are being reworked to allow some forward provisioning and relaxation of mark-to-market rules. International regulators have also been casting their minds more widely: they would like to design a financial system where bad shocks are dampened not exaggerated, and where the core parts stay stable. This is macro-financial management, an area where we have been active and continue to work. Our aim is to stabilise the financial system and help reduce the work that monetary policy might otherwise need to do.

Politicians and regulators will always take lessons from a crisis to avoid the same problems in the future; banks will always seek creative ways to try to avoid such regulation. But the next crisis, of course, will be different.

At the end of 2009, one of the international wire agencies was gathering regulators' views on the global financial crisis, and they asked me for some thoughts on New Zealand banking. I jotted down a few notes:

- New Zealand is on the other side of the world, but when nasty stuff happens there is no place to hide.
- New Zealand banks have been over-reliant on short-term international funding and this must change.
- Straightforward, vanilla-type banking in an economy such as New Zealand's is far safer than that of the complex international banking systems.
- The major Australasian banks came through the crisis well, because of good management, good regulation and good luck.
- Through the crisis our interests were usually the same as Australia's, but if things had worsened, our interests might have diverged.
- Bank regulation can be light-handed, but to be successful it needs to be hard-nosed.

- In self-interest, banks may encourage New Zealanders to take on more debt than is good for them individually or deliver more external liability than is good for the country.
- New Zealand needs bank credit to recover and grow.

New Zealand was comparatively lucky during the crisis. We had no bank collapses, no big government bailouts, no nasty scars. But we have no cause to be smug: it was not by our cleverness that we survived.

The crisis was not yet over when suggestions and advice about how to reform bank regulation began to avalanche down on us. But what about macro-economic policies? These have brought far less agreement and far fewer practical suggestions – and indeed, not everyone would see the crisis as having stemmed from any particular economic failure.

What did work reasonably well were reactive macro-stimulus policies: emergency liquidity, guarantees, intense monetary policy

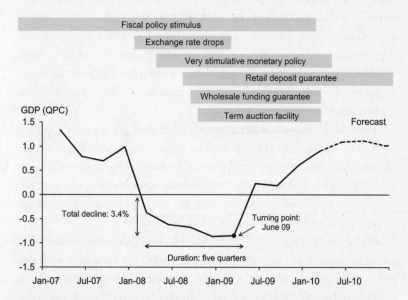

The stimulus measures had an effect: the diagram lists the various stimulus measures in a very simplified form. The timing of the recession is shown by the New Zealand GDP, measured in quarterly percentage change. For a more detailed description of the measures, see Alan Bollard, 'Handling our Economics Recovery', May 2010, available at www.rbnz.govt.nz.

stimulation, generic fiscal policies, specific government spending schemes, and some tax cuts and rebates. Academics now have real-world material to trawl through and analyse which should help provide guidelines on how to improve stimulus measures in the future.

Much more difficult is the macro-economic management needed to change the structural climate that contributed to the crisis and to avoid exposing ourselves to it again. How do we avoid the big international imbalances that built up over the last decade and the sectoral imbalances that emerged within particular countries? In New Zealand the challenge is to understand how we built up such a big balance of payments deficit, and why our household sector was so profligate while the business sector was more abstemious.

Classical macro-economists might expect rising global imbalances to be limited by, and recoveries to be assisted by, flexible changes in prices – whether it be the price of New Zealand dollars (exchange rates) or the price of capital (interest rates), or the terms of trade. Flows of trade and capital depend on these relative prices. But international distortions in these prices have persisted – and look like persisting into the future – driving countries to look at second-best ways around them, which can in turn increase the problem. Finding more appropriate ways to govern exchange rates and capital movements is a major challenge for the international economic community.

Meanwhile, there has been considerable thought about the policy tools available to central banks and to finance ministers. Traditionally conservative institutions like the IMF have suggested rethinking capital controls, inflation targeting and stabilisation policies. Forensic economists will have to rake through the ashes of the crisis before we can be clear about the appropriate economic lessons.

In the meantime, at the Reserve Bank we feel that inflation-targeting monetary policy has served us reasonably well. We have now endured some of the highest international price pressures, the worst international banking stress and the biggest international economic disruption of the post-World War II era. The inflation-targeting regime allowed us the flexibility we needed to stabilise the system through these shocks. Until better technologies come along, inflation targeting will remain the mainstay of our economic stabilisation. In the future it may be assisted by complementary macro-financial policies. We have learned that to be crisis-resilient an economy needs to be as balanced as possible. With its large savings and balance of payments deficits, New Zealand can hardly claim this.

To work effectively, a central bank's stabilisation policies also need to be in line with other domestic policies (such as tax and savings incentives), and we need big international countries themselves to run sensible monetary and exchange rate policies. Without that, we will be buffeted by whatever global winds blow our way.

New Zealand's economic position in the world remains hugely challenging. Over the long haul, our terms-of-trade trends look reasonably encouraging. But the crisis has shown that short-term fragilities can persist in a hostile world. As the crisis receded and the work pressures reduced, I was keen for the team at the Reserve Bank to learn from the experience. We asked an outsider to interview each member of our senior management team about their thoughts, worries, successes and fears through the crisis. From her report I concluded that we had been lucky to be working in a full-service central bank, which has huge advantages in sharing information and using different tools in a crisis. But we had to be careful not to raise expectations; there was a lot that we simply could not do. It had also been important to stay closer than usual to other parts of government through the crisis, and to the banks, while bearing in mind that too much closeness can breed over-dependence. In the midst of the crisis, we did our best to keep the big picture in mind and to look ahead, even if our real worries were about what would happen in the markets on Monday morning. It was a vital time to try to show leadership, but we were all short of sleep, foresight and energy.

We had a light-hearted diversion at Christmas 2009. A journalist contacted me to ask if I would review a strange new book. A New Zealand blogger, David Haywood, unknown to me, apparently a fan of childhood 'boys-own' type annuals, had produced a *New Zealand Reserve Bank Annual 2010*. He selected what he thought was one of New

Zealand's most boring establishments (the Reserve Bank) and one of Wellington's most boring establishment members (me), and subjected us to merciless satire.

This Alan Bollard was no quiet authority figure working through the crisis, but rather a screaming, ranting madman who resorted to violence (of the armed and unarmed variety) whenever he did not get his own way. It was more like a cross between Japanese manga comics and *Fear and Loathing in Las Vegas* than a boys-own annual. It had instructions for kids on how to be a central bank governor (complete with a cut-out Bollard mask), a five-minute crossword puzzle on macro-economics, a poetry corner devoted to verse about the CPI, and a story called 'A Night to Remember with Alan Bollard' (armed with a softball bat). After all we had been through, laughter was a welcome tonic.

During the year I had been invited to present a series of talks to business audiences about the global financial crisis. I wanted to give more than just a breathless recitation of events. First, I thought it important to list what we had learned about the effects of the global financial crisis on the world economy:

- The world's financial system and the world's economy are inextricably linked; a banking crisis hurts growth in the 'real' economy.
- Global imbalances can build up over a long period. Eventually rebalancing has to happen, and it may be costly – but if it does not happen things will hurt more.
- We rely on price signals (including exchange rates and interest rates) to guide major allocation decisions, but some of these signals can diverge from economic fundamentals for an extended time.
- There are lessons for the United States from the long period of loose monetary policy following the East Asian crisis, and lessons for East Asia about over-reliance on indebted Western consumers as the main drivers of their growth.

- Major monetary and fiscal stimulus has worked reasonably well to prevent further deterioration, far better than it did in the 1930s.
- Competitive stimulation, competitive capital controls and competitive exchange rate policy will ultimately hurt everyone.
- The global crisis has damaged the old northern countries much more than emerging markets and commodity producers, and this is changing the global economic balance of power.
- The disruptions are disguising some important long-term economic trends: emerging market growth, demand for commodities, demographic problems and global warming.
- We will need to see how the exits from stimulus measures work before we can judge the success of crisis management; so far the solutions are resulting in more expensive capital.

Having collected my thoughts, I still did not see a way to convey the complicated interaction of world markets to a general audience. But by chance I had been reading an article about bubonic plague in medieval Europe. The drama and lack of knowledge struck a chord. Some research on the internet soon confirmed that the plague might provide an interesting analogy to contemporary economic events.

Some 650 years ago virulent strains of bubonic plague, probably from China, landed in Europe, and within a year or two spread right across the continent. It was particularly destructive in Iceland and Ireland, where up to 60 per cent of the population contracted the bacteria and most of the infected died. Corpses lined the streets.

The authorities could not understand what caused or spread the disease. They tried to contain it by isolating ships and by burning infected houses, but, when they did, rats carrying the bacteria would escape, only to spread it further. Within several years, after immense disruption, sorrow and death, the disease gradually burned itself out, leaving devastation behind.

Occasional outbreaks of bubonic plague continued to occur for centuries in Europe and still do in poorer regions of the world. Improved public health reduced infection rates, but only in the early twentieth century were the causes of the disease isolated by improved clinical diagnosis. Even then, it was not till the development of the antibiotic streptomycin by a Ukrainian-American doctor, Selman Waksman, during World War II that this deadly bacteria could be contained.

The comparison with financial plague was irresistible: I called my series of talks 'Bring Out your Dead'. The new plague had spread from the United States (or, some might argue, again from China), rampantly infecting European domestic markets; within a year or two it had spread infection across money, equity, commodity, foreign exchange, capital and sovereign funding markets. It struck the financial systems of Ireland and Iceland particularly hard. Initially, diagnosis was tricky. The authorities did not understand what caused or spread the disease – they had thought that they had good principles of financial health in place. They tried to contain the outbreak by isolating institutions and guaranteeing funds, but the germs still spread.

Now the crisis is gradually burning itself out, but leaving disruption behind. Clinical researchers have tracked the causes back to the virulent germs of subprime and derivatives, exacerbated by unhygienic practices such as off-balance-sheet vehicles, originate-and-distribute models and poor governance, much of which went largely uncontrolled by financial health professionals.

Have we yet developed an antibiotic? Is there an economist equivalent of Dr Waksman, who developed streptomycin? Or could the plague return?

TIMELINE

WORLD	DATE	NEW ZEALAND
	1980s	Rogernomics reforms
Alan Greenspan becomes chairman of the US Federal Reserve	**1987**	
Share market crash		
The Great Moderation begins		
Basel I Accords	**1988**	Don Brash becomes governor of the Reserve Bank
	1989	Reserve Bank becomes world's first inflation targeter
Thailand stock market falls; Asian Financial Crisis	**1997**	
Hedge fund crisis; Long-Term Capital Management bailout	**1998**	Alan Bollard becomes secretary to the Treasury
'Y2K'	**1999**	Fifth Labour Government elected
		New Zealand dollar drops to US40 cents
US tech wreck	**2000**	
Alan Greenspan cuts cash rates by over 5%		
9/11 attacks	**2001**	
Enron files for bankruptcy		
Western housing markets on growth track	**2002**	Don Brash resigns; Alan Bollard becomes Reserve Bank governor
		Reserve Bank revises banking standards: large banks required to incorporate in New Zealand
Severe acute respiratory syndrome (SARS) epidemic	**2003**	Reserve Bank doubles holdings of notes
Avian influenza epidemic	**2004**	Beginning of nine OCR rises
Basel II Accords		Reserve Bank broadens its foreign exchange intervention policy
US banks giving high-risk subprime loans		
Ben Bernanke gives 'savings glut' speech	**2005**	
Oil prices hit US$60 a barrel		
Ben Bernanke appointed chairman of the Federal Reserve	**2006**	Finance companies begin to display problems

WORLD	DATE	NEW ZEALAND
New Century Financial files for Chapter 11 bankruptcy	**April 2007**	
Subprime crisis		
	July 2007	OCR hits record 8.25%
		Reserve Bank begins holding some foreign reserves in an 'unhedged' or 'open' position
BNP Paribus freezes two funds	**August 2007**	Reserve Bank accepts bank bills/bonds as security for lending to ensure banks have cash
Northern Rock fails; bank run ensues	**September 2007**	
UK Government guarantees Northern Rock deposits		
Federal Reserve starts cutting target Federal funds rate		
Oil prices hit US$100 by year-end	**December 2007**	
Maximum growth in derivative products		
President George W. Bush announces plans to assist US homeowners facing foreclosure		
Federal Reserve announces Term Auction Facility		
Five major central banks offer billions of dollars in loans to banks		
US dollar swap lines established		
Bond insurers' credit ratings downgraded		
Global stock markets' biggest falls since 9/11	**January 2008**	
Federal Reserve's biggest interest rate cuts in 25 years		
Bear Stearns is acquired by JPMorgan Chase with US Federal Reserve assistance	**March 2008**	
	May 2008	Reserve Bank announces new liquidity measures
		Basel II capital standard applies for New Zealand banks

WORLD	DATE	NEW ZEALAND
Federal Reserve rescue package for Fannie Mae and Freddie Mac	**July 2008**	OCR cut by 25 basis points to 8%
Crude oil futures hit an all-time high of US$147.27 a barrel		
US unemployment reaches 6.1%	**September 2008**	Reserve Bank becomes regulator of non-bank deposit takers
US Government takes Fannie Mae and Freddie Mac into conservatorship		OCR cut by 50 basis points to 7.5%
Lehman Brothers files for Chapter 11 bankruptcy		GDP figures for June show NZ in recession
AIG receives US$85 billion rescue package from Federal Reserve		Banks report increased withdrawals of $100 notes
Bank of America buys Merrill Lynch		
Goldman Sachs and Morgan Stanley become licensed bank holding companies		
Washington Mutual Bank closed by regulators, on-sold to JPMorgan Chase		
US Congress rejects first Troubled Asset Relief Program (TARP) plan		
Icelandic financial crisis begins		
Ireland guarantees bank deposits		
Bank takeovers and nationalisation in the US, UK, France		
UK, US apply quantitative easing measures to stabilise financial systems and encourage lending	**October 2008**	Reserve Bank allows residential mortgage-backed securities as collateral to ensure banks have cash
US Congress passes TARP bill		NZ general election announced
Reserve Bank of Australia cuts cash rates by 100 basis points		Retail Deposit Guarantee Scheme launched
Central banks in England, China, Canada, Sweden, Switzerland and European Central Bank join Federal Reserve in emergency interest rate cuts of 50 basis points		Crisis demand for cash stemmed
		NZ CPI rises 5.1% for the year
		OCR cut by 100 basis points to 6.5%
European, UK bank bailouts		US Federal Reserve and Reserve Bank of New Zealand establish temporary reciprocal currency arrangement (swap line)
Many countries guarantee retail deposits, including Australia		
Dow Jones index drops 8%		
World equity markets have now lost about half their value since beginning of year		

WORLD	DATE	NEW ZEALAND
IMF loans to Ukraine, Iceland	**November 2008**	Wholesale Guarantee Scheme launched
China Government's stimulus package		
Bank of England cuts rates by 150 points		General election; National Party coalition government formed
US presidential election		Reserve Bank provides Term Auction Facility (TAF) bill tenders
G-20 leaders meet		
US Government allocates record US$300 billion for Citibank rescue package		
Eurozone, US in recession	**December 2008**	OCR cut by 150 basis points to 5%
US interest rates cut to 0–0.25%		Current account deficit rises to 8.6% of GDP
Return on US three-month Treasury bonds goes negative		
US jobless rate 7.2%	**January 2009**	Reserve Bank accepts corporate- and asset-backed securities to support liquidity
Chinese exports suffer biggest fall in decade; New Year layoffs		
UK in recession		Standard & Poor's puts New Zealand credit rating on 'negative outlook'
Inauguration of US President Obama		OCR cut by 150 basis points to 3.5%
		Reserve Bank and Treasury officials take road show to market capitals
US Treasury Secretary Tim Geithner announces Financial Stability Plan	**February 2009**	Prime Minister John Key's Job Summit
	March 2009	NZ dollar hits US49 cents low
		Mascot Finance collapses; first claim on NZ Retail Deposit Guarantee Scheme
		OCR cut by 50 basis points to 3%
		Visit by International Monetary Fund
G-20 leaders meet; agree US$1.1 trillion measures	**April 2009**	OECD releases forecast for NZ
Fiji coup		OCR cut by 50 basis points to 2.5%
US Congress approves US$3.4 trillion budget to pay for rescue initiatives		
world outbreak of influenza A (H1N1)		

WORLD	DATE	NEW ZEALAND
Chrysler files for bankruptcy Ten US banks fail stress tests	**May 2009**	Reserve Bank releases liquidity policy to reduce dependence on short-term wholesale funding NZ economy reaches trough OCR unchanged at 2.5% Rising NZ dollar
General Motors files for bankruptcy World's oil consumption falls for first time in nearly two decades UK unemployment 7.1% OECD says world economy is near bottom of worst recession in post-war history Ten of largest US banks say able to repay government (TARP) loans Japanese economy experiences record decline in first quarter 2009 China's economy growing very strongly due to government's stimulation package Australians announce they have avoided recession	**June 2009**	Monetary Policy Statement points to first green shoots of recovery OCR unchanged at 2.5%
Goldman Sachs announces quarterly profit Meeting of East Asian and Pacific Reserve Bank governors in Hong Kong	**July 2009**	Reserve Bank report on banking to parliamentary Select Committee OCR unchanged at 2.5%
Ben Bernanke re-nominated as chair of Federal Reserve by President Obama	**August 2009**	Reserve Bank 75th Anniversary OCR unchanged at 2.5%
Sovereign debt crisis spreads; Dubai, Eastern Europe and PIIGS	**Late 2009–May 2010**	NZ out of recession Phasing out of emergency liquidity schemes
President Obama's healthcare legislation passed	**March 2010**	
	April 2010	Wholesale Guarantee Scheme ends
Greek sovereign debt crisis leads to bailout by IMF and European Union	**May 2010**	
	June 2010	OCR increased by 25 basis points to 2.75%

FURTHER READING

Ahamed, Liaquat, *Lords of Finance: The Bankers Who Broke the World*, Penguin Press, New York, 2009.

Cecchetti, Stephen G., M. S. Mohanty and Fabrizio Zampolli, 'The future of Public Debt: Prospects and Implications', BIS Working Paper No. 300, 2010, http://www.bis. org/publ/oth009.pdf

Davies, Howard and David Green, *Banking on the Future: The Fall and Rise of Central Banking*, Princeton University Press, Princeton, 2010.

Ferguson, Niall, *The Ascent of Money: A Financial History of the World*, Allen Lane, London, 2008.

Greenspan, Alan, *The Age of Turbulence: Adventures in a New World*, Penguin Press, New York, 2007.

Lewis, Michael, *The Big Short: Inside the Doomsday Machine*, W. W. Norton & Co., New York, 2010.

Paulson, Henry M., *On the Brink: Inside the Race to Stop the Collapse of the Global Financial System*, Business Plus, New York, 2010.

Posner, Richard A., *A Failure of Capitalism: The Crisis of '08 and the Descent into Depression*, Harvard University Press, Cambridge, MA, 2009.

Reinhart, Carmen M. and Kenneth S. Rogoff, *This Time Is Different: Eight Centuries of Financial Folly*, Princeton University Press, Princeton, 2009.

Reserve Bank of New Zealand, *Monetary Policy Statements*, quarterly, http://www.rbnz. govt.nz/monpol/statements/

Reserve Bank of New Zealand, *Financial Stability Reports*, six-monthly, http://www. rbnz.govt.nz/finstab/fsreport/

Reserve Bank of New Zealand and the New Zealand Treasury, *Supplementary Stabilisation Instruments (SSI) Report*, 2006, http://www.rbnz.govt.nz/monpol/about/2452274.pdf

Roubini, Nouriel and Stephen Mihm, *Crisis Economics: A Crash Course in the Future of Finance*, Penguin Press, New York, 2010.

Sorkin, Andrew R., *Too Big to Fail: The Inside Story of How Wall Street and Washington Fought to Save the Financial System – and Themselves*, Allen Lane, Sydney, 2009.

Soros, George, *The Crash of 2008 and What it Means: The New Paradigm for Financial Markets*, PublicAffairs Book, New York, 2009.

Stewart, James B., 'Eight Days', *The New Yorker*, 21 September 2009, pp. 58–81.

Stiglitz, Joseph E., *Freefall: America, Free Markets, and the Sinking of the World Economy*, W. W. Norton & Co., New York, 2010.

Tett, Gillian, *Fool's Gold: How the Bold Dream of a Small Tribe at J. P. Morgan was Corrupted by Wall Street Greed and Unleashed a Catastrophe*, Free Press, New York, 2009.

Wessel, David, *In Fed We Trust: Ben Bernanke's War on the Great Panic*, Crown Business, New York, 2009.

Wolf, Martin, *Fixing Global Finance*, Johns Hopkins University Press, Baltimore, MD, 2008.

INDEX

Page numbers in *italics* refer to captions and figures.

New Zealand Symphony Orchestra, 151
New Zealand Treasury, 6, 23, 27, 39, 45–46, 60, 61, 63, 63, 74–75, 81, 88, 106–7, 113, 120, 113, 139–41, 150, 159, 166, 189, 192
Niemeyer, Otto, 169
non-banks, 24, 29, 65, 165–66, 130, 191; *see also* finance companies; credit unions; building societies
Northern Rock, 32, 45, 60, 190

Obama, Barack, 71, 96, 102–3, 111, 138, 172, 178, 192–93
Oddsson, David, 97
Office of the Comptroller of the Currency, 118
official cash rate (OCR), 21, 28, 38–39, 45, 47–48, 72, 73, 82, 85–86, 102, 104–5, 121–22, 124, 141, 143, 145–48, 153–154, 161, 164, 189–93; *see also* Reserve Bank of New Zealand, advisory groups, OCR Advisory Group
oil:
   consumption, 14, 139, 193
   New Zealand as exporter, 16–17
   prices, 5, 9, 14–17, 21, 28, 35, 38, 72, 78, 189–91
OPEC, 5
Organisation for Economic Co-operation and Development (OECD), 20, 82, *93*, 127, 139, 146, 152, 169, 175, 192–93
Orr, Adrian, 25

Pacific Islands, 120, 125, 167, 174, 193
Parliamentary Select Committees, 120–21, 125, 148–49, 164, 193
Paulson, Henry, 33, 42–43, 49–51, 71
payment and settlement systems, 51–52, 87, 103, 114, 158, 163; *see also* Reserve Bank of New Zealand
Peters, Winston, 80
Phillips curve, 39
Phillips, A. W. H. (Bill), 39, 132
PIIGS, 99, 109, 176–77, 193
Plunket, Sean, 115
Policy Targets Agreement (RBNZ), 16, 21, 38, 94

Portugal, 99, *177*; *see also* PIIGS
Premier House, 144
Primary Fund, 53
press, 22, 38, 48, 57, 66, 73, 78, 94, 124–25, 146, 161; *see also* media
Public Finance Act, 64, 74, 101

Queen Elizabeth II, 169

radio, 48, 77, 79, 115, 126; *see also* media
Rajan, Raghuram, 3
recession, late 2000s: in New Zealand, 6, 19, 57, 84–85, 104, 106, 115, 122, 135, 140, 145, 150, 169, 179, *183*, 191; in other countries, 40, 81, 97, 104, 108, 119, 125, 127, 136, *138*, 152, 192–93
Reinhart, Carmen, 170, 175
Reis, Ricardo, 2
Reserve Bank Act, 25
Reserve Bank of Australia, 38, 56, 58, 78, 133, 191
Reserve Bank of Fiji, 125–26
Reserve Bank of New Zealand (RBNZ):
   advisory groups: Board of Directors, 23–24, 38, 47, 56, 67, 72, 75, 94, 113, 132, 150, 161; Crisis Advisory Group, 114; OCR Advisory Group, 39, 122, 145–46 *passim* (*see also* official cash rate)
   balance sheet, 28, 43–45, 100, 113, 121, 132, 161–63, 180
   conferences: 75th anniversary, 169–70; A. W. H. (Bill) Phillips' 50th anniversary, 39
   econometric models, 81, 87, 122, 132, 139, 142, 145
   foreign exchange (FX) dealings, 23–24, 28, 44, 91, 102, 121, 127, 153, 161–63, 169, 190; *see also* Term Auction Facilities
   publications, *see Financial Stability Report*; *Monetary Policy Statement*
   roles and responsibilities: as full-service central bank, 21, 23–27, 29–30, 37–38, 51, 52, 72–73, 75, 185, 130, 159, 166; of governor, 23, 38; *see also*

terms of trade, 6, 16, 174, 184–85
Thailand, 3–4, 189
Think Big, 6
Timaru, 67
Tokyo, 163
Trentham Racecourse, 35
Trichet, Jean-Claude, 97
Troubled Asset Relief Programme
    (TARP), 54–55, 71, 152, 157, 191, 193
Tyler, Simon, 44–45, 76, 89, 114, 121; *see
    also* Reserve Bank of New Zealand,
    staff, teams and departments,
    financial markets department

UBS, 33, 109
Ukraine, 81, 109, 176, 192
unemployment: in New Zealand, 6, 19,
    113, 115, 153; in other countries, 85, 96,
    98–99, 110, 139, 174–75, 178, 191, 193
United Kingdom (UK), 12, 32, 55, 127, 151,
    159–60, 70, 82, 101, 138, 165, 177, 182,
    190–92; *see also* currencies, pound
    sterling
United States:
    auto industry, 69, 82, 121, 137, 171; *see also*
        Chrysler; Ford; General Motors
    banks, 52, 159, 189, 193; *see also* United
        States Federal Reserve; Federal
        Reserve Bank of New York; *names of
        individual banks*
    Congress, *see* United States,
        Government
    dollar, *see* currencies, US dollar
    Government, 30, 42, 54–55, 58, 71–74,
        96, 112, 118, 137, 140, 159–60, 172,
        191–92
    presidential election, 2008, 55, 71–72,
        74, 78, 192
    Treasury, 33, 42, 55, 70–72, 90, 102,
        111–12, 118, 137–38, 152, 164, 192
    White House's National Economic
        Council, 72
    US dollar swap facility, 34, 73–74, 100,
        190–91

United States Federal Reserve (Fed),
    1–3, 9, 11, 13, 21, 30, 33–34, 36–37, 39,
    42–43, 49–50, 53–54, 58, 70–73, 118,
    135, 163, 170, 72, 189–91, 193; *see also*
    Federal Reserve Bank of New York
    (New York Fed)
Uruguay Round, 3
US tech wreck, 6, 189

Wachovia Bank, 54
Waksman, Selman, 188
Wall Street Journal, 172
Wall Street, 10, 19, 33, 36, 42–43, 47–51, 54,
    59, 64, 107, 111–12
Washington Mutual Bank, 54, 191
Washington, 20, 39, 42, 47, 61, 70, 82, 92,
    118, 120
Watson, Mark, 2
Wellington Anniversary Day, 35
Wellington, 35, 77, 85, 103, 115, 117, 120, 132
Westpac, 18
Wevers, Maarten, 48, 56
Whale Rider, 73
White House, 70, 72
White, Bill, 160
White, Harry Dexter, 71, 136
Whitehead, John, 45–46, 56, 61, 74, 79,
    81, 103, 106, 113, 115, 124; *see also* New
    Zealand Treasury
Wholesale Guarantee Schemes: New
    Zealand, 76, 131, 152, 163, 180, 192–93;
    Australia, 76, 131
Wilson, Bill, 23
Wilson, Mary, 48
Wolyncewicz, Mike, 87
World Bank, 173
World Economic Outlook, 120
World Health Organisation (WHO), 142
World Trade Organization, 3

Year 2000 problem (Y2K), 6, 189

Zhou Xiaochuan, 98, 112